Academic Planning for the 1980s

Richard B. Heydinger
Guest Editor

Jossey-Bass Inc., Publishers
San Francisco • Washington • London

LB
2361.5
.A25

ACADEMIC PLANNING FOR THE 1980s
New Directions for Institutional Research
Volume VII, Number 4, 1980
  Richard B. Heydinger, Guest Editor

Copyright © 1980 by Jossey-Bass Inc., Publishers
     and
    Jossey-Bass Limited

Copyright under International, Pan American, and Universal
Copyright Conventions. All rights reserved. No part of
this issue may be reproduced in any form—except for brief
quotation (not to exceed 500 words) in a review or professional
work—without permission in writing from the publishers.

New Directions for Institutional Research (publication number
USPS 098-830) is published quarterly by Jossey-Bass Inc., Publishers,
and is sponsored by the Association for Institutional Research.
Subscriptions are available at the regular rate for institutions,
libraries, and agencies of $30 for one year. Individuals may
subscribe at the special professional rate of $18 for one year.
New Directions is numbered sequentially—please order extra
copies by sequential number. The volume and issue numbers
above are included for the convenience of libraries.

Correspondence:
Subscriptions, single-issue orders, change of address notices,
undelivered copies, and other correspondence should be sent to
New Directions Subscriptions, Jossey-Bass Inc., Publishers,
433 California Street, San Francisco, California 94104.

Editorial correspondence should be sent to the Editor-in-Chief,
Marvin W. Peterson, Center for the Study of Higher Education,
University of Michigan, Ann Arbor, Michigan 48109.

Library of Congress Catalogue Card Number LC 79-92032
International Standard Serial Number ISSN 0271-0579
International Standard Book Number ISBN 87589-840-8

Cover design by Willi Baum
Manufactured in the United States of America

Contents

Introduction: Academic Program Planning in Perspective   Richard B. Heydinger   1

It must be recognized that each institution has an existing planning style, and new approaches to academic planning must take into account institutionalized planning practices.

Needs as a Basis for Academic Program Planning   Oscar T. Lenning   9

Although needs assessment is a viable tool to assist administrators and faculty members concerned about meeting client and community needs for programs, more development in this area must take place before it can begin to reach its full potential.

Using Institutional Data to Plan Academic Programs — A Case History   Thomas M. Freeman   27
William A. Simpson

A case history that recounts the evolutionary development of a unified evaluation, budgeting, and planning system at Michigan State University over a period of eight years—a system that is strongly based upon the collection and analysis of department, college, and institutional data.

Resource Reallocation: Stopgap or Support for Academic Planning?   R. Sue Mims   57

When real resources decline, demands change, or programs lose vitality, then a logical move is to reallocate resources to facilitate academic planning.

The Roles of Incentives in Academic Planning   Stephen A. Hoenack   73
David J. Berg

Attempts to plan or budget without considering the behavioral effects of existing or proposed incentives will produce unintended, and possibly undesirable, results.

Academic Program Planning Reconsidered   Richard B. Heydinger   97

The conditions facing postsecondary education during the 1980s call for institutional planning styles that are comprehensive, systematic, public, regular, and expansive.

Further Sources on Academic Planning   Richard B. Heydinger   111

Index   115

The Association for Institutional Research was created in 1966 to benefit, assist, and advance research leading to improved understanding, planning, and operation of institutions of higher education. Publication policy is set by its Publication Board.

PUBLICATIONS BOARD
Gerald W. McLaughlin (Chairperson), Virginia Polytechnic Institute and State University
Alfred A. Cooke, Institute for Service to Education, Washington, D.C.
John A. Lucas, William Rainey Harper College, Palatine, Illinois
Marilyn McCoy, National Center for Higher Education Management Systems, Boulder, Colorado
Marvin W. Peterson, University of Michigan
Joan S. Stark, University of Michigan

EX-OFFICIO MEMBERS OF THE PUBLICATION BOARD
Mary E. Corcoran, University of Minnesota
Charles Elton, University of Kentucky
Douglas Mathewson, University of Nevada
Richard R. Perry, University of Toledo

EDITORIAL ADVISORY BOARD
All members of the Publications Board and:
Frederick E. Balderson, University of California, Berkeley
Howard R. Bowen, Claremont Graduate School
Roberta D. Brown, Arkansas College
Robert M. Clark, University of British Columbia
Lyman A. Glenny, University of California, Berkeley
David S. P. Hopkins, Stanford University
Roger G. Schroeder, University of Minnesota
Robert J. Silverman, Ohio State University
Martin A. Trow, University of California, Berkeley

Each institution has an existing planning style, and new approaches to academic planning must take into account institutionalized planning practices.

Introduction: Academic Program Planning in Perspective

Richard B. Heydinger

As our society has become more complex, more interdependent, and more technological, it is understandable that as a culture we would increasingly attempt to control our destinies. Thus over the past two decades there has been a growing emphasis on planning and how organizations might better adapt to the future. As with other segments of society, postsecondary education has felt the need to improve its planning capabilities. With resources growing tighter and student enrollments predicted to decline significantly, even reluctant academic academic administrators have responded to the pressure by initiating formal planning processes, hoping that these will aid them in making the difficult choices facing their institutions.

Because of these developments, a sizable body of literature has been produced on planning in colleges and universities; however, little has been written which focuses exclusively on planning academic programs. Although over the centuries a great deal has been written on the curriculum and its organization, there is a paucity of literature on approaches (that is, processes) for planning academic programs. In the 1980s, the effective planning of academic programs, which may be regarded as the cornerstone of an institution, will in large part determine the future of a college or university. Already decisions are being forced on academic administrators which necessitate the investment in one program at the sacrifice of another. Well-developed approaches to academic program planning cannot substitute for good judgment and keen insight. However, an effective planning process can increase the likelihood that fundamental academic values are considered and that the institution remains vital throughout this difficult period.

The Topic

Although a precise definition of planning is difficult, it is possible to note the characteristics that today are generally associated with planning. As one author has said, "The central goal of planning is not a blueprint but a series of generalized guides to future decisions and actions" (Kahn, 1969). Peter Drucker, the doyen of management theory, focuses on the "futurity" of present decisions, noting that any of today's decisions which affect tomorrow are in essence planning (Drucker, 1972). Thus, planning is future oriented. It is a specification of a desired state the institution is striving to attain. It is also rational; and to whatever extent advisable, planning decisions are data based. This is not to say that planning is deterministic and that numbers are simply plugged into equations. Instead, planning is a process that builds on available evidence and attempts to embrace the future through rational decision making. Thus, contemporary notions of planning contain the following characteristics: a future orientation, rational decision making, and a focus on process rather than product.

For the purposes of this volume, *academic programs* are defined as the instructional component of a college or university. This definition encompasses graduate and undergraduate instruction, as well as degree and nondegree programs. The organizational focal point of academic programs is the academic department. Academic support services, physical planning, and other aspects of the institution are not directly considered in this volume. Stated another way, the planning of academic programs usually falls under the purview of the academic department, the college, and the office of academic affairs. The offices of finance, administration, support services, research, development, and institutional relations represent other important aspects of the college or university. Typically, however, they are not directly involved in planning academic programs.

The reader should recognize that this volume does not discuss all aspects of academic program planning. For example, the planning of individual courses is not the reference point for these authors. Instead, the unit of analysis is the academic department and the degree programs which it offers. This volume does encompass an institutionwide perspective on academic program planning; however, these discussions do not go beyond the institutional level. For example, the increasingly important role which state agencies are playing in program planning is not discussed. This is not to say that these dimensions of program planning are unimportant, but space does not permit an exhaustive examination of them.

The reader is cautioned against thinking that academic program planning is a new venture. The planning of instructional offerings has been taking place since formal education began. Yet, due to the emphasis on rational decision making and comprehensive planning, new approaches to academic planning have been developed and implemented. Thus today it is possible to cite at least thirteen different styles used to plan academic programs (see Figure 1). Some of these styles are as old as schooling itself (knowledge development), while others are relatively new (formal democratic) and reflect the development of new technologies (program data) or the need to respond to "market" conditions (needs assessment). In some way all of these styles currently play an important role in planning academic programs in American postsecondary education. Most importantly, it must be recognized and emphasized that each institution has a planning style in place today. Somehow programs are planned, and changes are made to existing degree programs. Before proposing a change, the wise institutional researcher will first identify and consider the existing planning style of the institution.

These thirteen styles are cited to set the context for this *New Directions* volume and to demonstrate that only a few approaches to academic planning are discussed herein. The term *style* was chosen because it connotes the impreciseness inherent in planning academic programs. Terms such as *methodology, system,* or *model* all imply a structured series of events which does not characterize most academic program planning.

Although this taxonomy may imply that these planning approaches are mutually exclusive, they are not. In reality the planning style of an institution is made up of elements from a number of styles. In designing changes, the most effective planning approach will be one that is tailored to the institution and draws upon a number of these styles. Yet for the purposes of diagnosing the existing planning process or designing a new one, this taxonomy may prove beneficial.

As implied in the brief descriptions in Figure 1, these styles can be contrasted along with a number of dimensions. For example, some styles (knowledge development, entrepeneurial) wait for faculty initia-

Figure 1. A Taxonomy of Styles for Planning Academic Programs

- *Knowledge Development*—curriculum development occurs as an unintentional by-product of research. For example, the discipline of computer science was added to the curriculum after the initial research on digital computing.

- *Entrepreneurial*—a laissez faire, individual approach to program planning which relies on faculty members to come forward whenever they have an idea for altering or expanding academic programs. There are no planning constraints, no timetables, no formal requests for ideas.

- *Administrative Initiative*—program planning ideas originate with academic administration which then may follow a variety of actions to have these plans implemented.

- *Curriculum Committee*—program development is either initiated or reviewed by a committee of faculty.

- *Governing/Coordinating Board*—the responsibility and initiative for planning and reviewing academic programs rests with the institution's governing board (trustees, Regents, for example) or the state's coordinating board.

- *Formal Democratic*—a cyclic planning process in which all units are requested to formulate their plans for program development. Plans are reviewed simultaneously to arrive at an overall academic plan for the department, college, university, or system. (See Chapter Six)

- *Program Focused*—planning of programs is conducted on an "as needed" basis—whenever a problem arises or a unique opportunity presents itself. Responsibility for initiating this process may rest with a number of constituencies, including some external to the institution.

- *Needs Assessment*—planning academic programs is guided by the needs of students, alumni, or employers. This information is collected through any number of social science research techniques. (See Chapter Two)

- *Program Data*—the collection and collation of a comprehensive set of measures reflecting the current status and trends of academic programs. Such data are typically maintained by the office of institutional research and used by academic administration to guide program planning decisions. (See Chapter Three)

- *Program Review*—a retrospective process which assesses the strengths and weaknesses of existing academic programs as a means for suggesting program development and improvement.

- *Program Development Fund*—through a formal process of submitting proposals, ideas for program development are selected and awarded funds for implementation. This institutional process is analogous to applying for a grant from a private foundation.

- *Incremental Budgeting*—the traditional budgeting process through which most academic program planning decisions are made. Recently special procedures for "retrenchment and reallocation" have been developed as part of this approach to program planning. (See Chapters Three and Four)

- *Economic Incentives*—with the institution viewed as an economic organization, an incentive structure is created which rewards particular types of activities. Each individual faculty member or unit selects programs to be developed on the basis of its response to the existing incentive structure. (See Chapter Five)

Note: For a more detailed description of these thirteen academic planning styles and a discussion of their contrasts, see Heydinger (in press).

tive before developing new programs. With these styles only those faculty who push for change are directly involved in the planning. In contrast, an institutionwide approach to planning (formal democratic) requires that all departments prepare plans on a regular schedule. Although in this style the source of ideas rests with faculty (as it should), the administration is responsible for ensuring that this process is executed in a timely manner. Some of these planning styles (program review, program data, formal democratic, incremental budgeting) have built in calenders, whereas some approaches (problem focused, knowledge development) do not take action until people come forward with a need. In a subtle way some styles favor the planning of new programs (program development fund, entrepreneurial), whereas other styles are weighted to favor the status quo (program review, incremental budgeting), because they focus on existing programs or demand participation by a large portion of the faculty. After all, in most cases human beings would rather perpetuate the status quo than introduce a change. Although space does not permit a full discussion of the differences among these planning styles (interested readers should consult Heydinger, in press), these characteristics must be carefully weighed by institutional researchers as they contemplate changes to their existing planning approaches. A particular planning style must be congruent with the philosophy, mission, and leadership style of the institution as it currently exists.

Guide to Following Chapters

Four planning styles have been singled out for discussion in this volume. Although all thirteen styles merit serious consideration, these four approaches were selected because their characteristics are most appropriate for the conditions which postsecondary education will face during the 1980s. These chapters are intended to provide the institutional researcher with a practical guide to academic program planning. Most of this volume is based on actual experiences, from which, it is hoped, we can learn.

One of the most widely used approaches to program planning is *program review*. Earlier this year an issue of New Directions for Institutional Research was devoted to this topic (see Craven, 1980), and it was therefore excluded from discussion in this issue. Nevertheless, it should be recognized as an important planning style for the 1980s.

The first planning style presented is needs assessment (Chapter Two). Postsecondary education, particularly community colleges, has increasingly asked students and potential employers to define their educational needs. Many coordinating and governing boards specify that the "need" must be demonstrated before a new program can be approved. Oscar Lenning's comprehensive treatment of this methodology encompasses a definition of need, an examination of the origin of the need, a series of methodological suggestions, and an extensive bibliography. As institutions cast about to serve unmet needs in order to sustain enrollments, needs assessment will come to play an increasingly important role in academic planning.

Chapter Three discusses the use of program data in academic planning. During the growth decade of the 1960s, administrators emphasized the need for better management information to keep pace with the rapidly expanding environment. Not coincidentally, the introduction of the computer and its capabilities offered a technological fix for satisfying some of these needs. As a result many institutions set out to establish comprehensive management information systems. Naturally, much of the emphasis in developing these systems was focused on those growth segments which were most easily measurable: enrollment, student credit hours, revenues, expenses, and faculty size. In many institutions the data which are collated by these computer systems have been the guiding force in academic planning decisions. In a case history format Thomas Freeman and William Simpson trace the evolution of Michigan State University's Annual Evaluation and Review process, which is in part built on an elaborate set of data tables for each academic department. The numerous examples and summary recommendations which the authors provide should be most useful for those seeking practical guidance.

In addition to the focus on program data, the planning style employed at Michigan State has characteristics of the formal democratic and incremental budgeting styles. Through this case history approach, the authors demonstrate that the most effective planning style must develop with the needs of the institution and will most certainly have characteristics of a number of styles.

Chapter Four focuses on one aspect of incremental budgeting, retrenchment and reallocation. Perhaps no term in today's educational lexicon is more hackneyed than "retrenchment and reallocation," yet R&R has become the primary process by which many institutions establish their academic priorities. Because this modification of the institution's budgeting process seems destined during the next decade to have a major influence on programmatic decisions, it cannot be overlooked as an academic planning style. For those institutions that have resisted the institutionalization of an ongoing planning process, budgeting is often the sole source of decisions on academic programs. Even for those institutions with formal planning processes, many are seeking the Holy Grail which will link budgeting to planning, and the R&R process offers a temporary solution. In this chapter R. Sue Mims describes the different approaches to R&R used by two research universities, Michigan and Oklahoma State. These contrasting case studies offer the reader a basis for useful comparisons with the practices at their own institutions.

Chapter Five discusses the use of economic incentives as a style for academic planning. The ultimate test of any planning process is whether the people and the organization are able to realize their desired outcomes, given the constraints of the environment. In this chapter Stephen Hoenack and David Berg present a provocative argument that incentives influence behavior within academic institutions, whether or not this influence is intended. The authors argue that if incentives are ignored, academic and organizational planning will have unintended, and perhaps undesired outcomes. This planning approach, which is built on the economic assumption of rational behavior and scarce resources, suggests that academic planning should motivate faculty and departments to act in a manner that will increase the achievement of broad organizational goals related to efficiency and academic quality. Although this approach has been described in a number of published articles, it has not received the attention it deserves, perhaps because the literature is laden with economic terminology that some people find difficult to understand. The effort expended in attempting to understand this material may be well rewarded. Yet some practitioners are skeptical of this planning style, noting that it has theoretical validity but few practical uses. In their chapter Hoenack and Berg explore the reasons why incentives are implicit in any planning and budgeting system, describe the potential for altering incentives in desirable ways, and propose a series of research studies to understand further the possibilities of this approach.

The final chapter highlights the distinctive characteristics of these four planning styles. In addition, the formal democratic style is singled out for further discussion. In this overview, Richard Heydinger attempts to stand back from the variety of approaches and contrast their philosophical assumptions and operational implications. Some suggestions are also provided on the general use of academic program planning approaches in the 1980s.

The chapter-by-chapter organization of this sourcebook has one inherent danger: namely, academic program planning will be seen as a formal, well-defined process. Although there are distinct approaches that can be delineated, the planning of academic programs in most institutions is a process which is a blend of these various styles. Also, it must be recognized that academic program planning occurs every day throughout a college or university. It occurs in the office of every faculty member as he or she makes decisions about course content. It occurs in the academic department when the faculty members decide on the sequencing of courses. It occurs in the office of academic affairs when the vice-president, provost, or dean decides which programs will receive discretionary funds. And it occurs at the state coordinating board when that board reviews existing programs for duplication.

The effective administrator and institutional researcher will recognize these various planning styles and their unique strengths and weaknesses. Different institutions require different approaches; different issues call for different styles. In dealing with academic program planning, we must never lose sight of the philosophy and purposes which undergird our particular institution. If after reading this volume, academic program planning is difficult to distinguish from many other day-to-day activities, then you have grasped the underlying theme of this volume. Yet if you see all activities as academic planning, then these writings have failed to communicate the importance and uniqueness of the activity.

References

Craven, E. (Ed.). *New Directions for Institutional Research: Academic Program Evaluation*, no. 27. San Francisco: Jossey-Bass, 1980.

Drucker, P. F. "Long-Range Planning Means Risk Taking." In D. W. Ewing (Ed.), *Long-Range Planning for Management*. New York: Harper & Row, 1972.

Heydinger, R. B. "Planning Academic Programs." In P. Jedamus and M. Peterson (Eds.), *Improving Academic Management: A Handbook of Planning and Institutional Research*. San Francisco: Jossey-Bass, in press.

Kahn, A. *Theory and Practice of Social Planning*. New York: Russell Sage Foundation, 1969.

Richard B. Heydinger is assistant to the vice-president for academic affairs at the University of Minnesota; he is on partial leave for three years as a Kellogg Fellow to study higher education planning and its relationship to long-range planning in other sectors of society.

Although needs assessment is a viable tool to assist administrators and faculty members concerned about meeting client and community needs for programs, more development in this area must take place before it can begin to reach its full potential.

Needs as a Basis for Academic Program Planning

Oscar T. Lenning

All instructional programs presumably exist to meet student needs, although some would claim that it is as much the needs of the provider (for financial support, for nonpecuniary benefits such as status and prestige, for survival, for growth, and so on) as of the students that motivates managers of some instructional programs. The concept of need is clearly an integral part of our culture. Most of the great literary classics are built around needs and how they are or are not met. Satisfying important human needs is therefore the central theme of almost all educational jargon.

Given that the concept of need is a driving force within education, including postsecondary education, the focus naturally turns to the analysis of which needs are most important, which are most feasible to meet, and which should receive priority attention in determining how available program funds and other resources (such as staff, facilities, and instructional methodologies) should be expended. And during a period of projected enrollment decline and probable financial retrench-

This chapter is a modified version of "A Conceptual Framework for Identifying and Assessing Needs," a paper presented at the Association for Instructional Research Annual Forum, Houston, May 22, 1978.

ment, an objective analysis of needs of enrolled students, prospective students, employers, the local community, and so forth becomes especially important for discerning which curricular programs to maintain, which to modify and how, which to cut back or eliminate, and which to start up. (Just because there is fiscal retrenchment does not mean that it is inappropriate to develop new programs; in fact, new programs that meet important needs and build on one's major strengths may be even more crucial at such a time.)

This chapter will focus on the identification and assessment of instructional programs needs. As will become clear, there are serious problems with such *needs assessment,* as it has come to be known, but such problems can be overcome. It is only during the last several years that college and university educators, other than those in the community colleges, have expressed much interest in conducting formal, objective studies to identify and assess needs. Fortunately, however, since the middle sixties, educators at the elementary and secondary levels have developed a significant body of knowledge about needs assessment from which postsecondary educators can borrow. In addition, important work that can be helpful in education has taken place in the field of human services (Baumheier and Heller, 1974). Furthermore, noteworthy developmental work is also now taking place in postsecondary education.

The demand for systematic, objective, and concrete needs assessment information will undoubtedly increase as rational planning models become more widely used within postsecondary education. The ability to assess needs objectively and to translate them effectively into institutional and program responses is expected to become increasingly important in the years ahead.

The Concept of Need

A major problem in the area of needs assessment has been the lack of a good definition of need. Conceptions of need that are expressed in the literature are not consistent, and often they are vague and nonspecific. Almost all needs assessment models have used a *discrepancy* definition, but as illustrated by Coffing and Hutchinson (1974), such a definition is too limited in its focus. Scriven (1977) cites the problem in colorful terms: "Needs assessments have been for some time the most ludicrous spectacle in evaluation. The usual 'models' are farcical and decisions based on them are built on soluble sand. One sign of the extent of the problem is the failure to begin with a tolerable definition of need . . . . Is a need a discrepancy between the actual and the ideal (a formula I used to like)? No, because we often need to improve and know how to, without knowing what the ideal would be like. There is some attraction about adding the requirement that *x* must be feasible, since it seems odd to say that one could need something that wasn't possible. But that would eliminate the motivation for . . . medical breakthroughs" (p. 25).

Needs are viewed in different ways by educators in various disciplines. For example, in the fields of biology, physiology, and medicine, needs are interpreted in terms of what will contribute to the efficient and effective functioning, survival, and growth of the human organism. Educators also tend to view needs in terms of individuals, but the focus here is more often on effective and efficient functioning, survival, and growth within the community or society. In psychology, needs are largely interpreted in terms of the perceptions of individuals. Psychologists usually view needs as a learned construct (taught or based on natural experience), the use of which is to indicate a perception of disequilibrium or unsatisfactory condition for which pressure (need) exists to right the situation. Another way to state this is that need is a personal tension and a means appropriate for meeting a desirable goal or condition, as perceived by an individual. Some psychologists would broaden this to include groups of people, and they construe a need as a force that pressures a person or a group to reduce or eliminate the discrepancy between what is perceived as desired and what perceptions or experiences indicate is currently the case. Sociologists, in turn, focus more on groups and society. They see needs as indicators of problems that must be solved, types and levels of competence that must be attained, and roles (and their integration) that must be carried out in order for individuals, groups, and organizations to function effectively as social units, and within a social community or society at large.

All of the above are legitimate types of needs that must be included in any generic definition of needs for use in postsecondary education, and aspects of each could be included in the concept of curricular program needs. The discrepancy definition of need guiding almost all formal needs assessment efforts and models up until now — the amount of discrepancy or gap that must be filled, through increased fulfillment or lowered thresholds of desirability, in order to bring the actual level of fulfillment (in terms of processes, procedures, conditions, outcomes, or results) up to the ideal level or condition — does not meet this condition. Neither does Coffing and Hutchinson's (1974) proposed alternative that need is a desired condition or state that may or may not be the current condition. Scriven (1977) — also bothered by the commonly accepted discrepancy concept of need — proposed a formula as a definition: "z needs x = z would (or does) significantly benefit from x, *and* z is now (or could be without x) in an unsatisfactory condition"

(p. 25). To illustrate this definition, let us suppose that z represents a college student, and x represents the particular knowledge and skills necessary to obtain a job. If we say that the student needs the knowledge and skills in order to obtain a job, we mean that: (1) The student would (or does) significantly benefit from the knowledge and skills, and (2) The student is now (or would be, without the knowledge and skills) in an unsatisfactory condition.

Scriven's definition adds important new clarifications, as he points out in his rationale: "at least it avoids the usual fallacies of a definition—explicit or implicit—of needs in terms of wants or preferences (children may need a cavity filled but they certainly don't want it done; conversely, people may think they need laetrile or CAI with Braille keys but it doesn't follow that they do.) Do you need a million dollars? No. Would you significantly benefit from it? Yes. Hence we can't omit the second clause in the definition, which reminds us that needs are (typically) necessities not luxuries" (P. 25). Scriven makes the important point that wants or preferences are not the same thing as needs. Needs may be present but unrecognized because of lack of knowledge, because the need is being fulfilled and there is no discrepancy, or because it is being masked by other needs that demand attention. Similarly, a person may want something merely to prevent someone else's having it. A want in such a case may be an expression of needs, but not the need expressed directly by the want (the expressed need is not the real need). Therefore, those conducting needs assessments are incorrect when the equate opinions, expressed desires, wants, or demands with needs. This is not to negate the usefulness of such information, which may provide good indications of needs that are present, especially if the wants are referred to by respondents in severe and critical terms (Taylor and others, 1974). But equating wants to needs causes people not to look for other types of information that could confirm whether those wants are valid and reliable indicators of need.

All of the definitions mentioned are legitimate concepts of need, and each defines a particular kind of need. Thus, what is called for is a definition that is broad or generic enough to include all of those specific types of need and show how they relate to one another. Lenning and others (1979) have proposed a definition of need that they believe has some validity in this respect: "A need is a necessary or desirable condition, state, or situation—whether it be an end result that is actuality (met need) or a discrepancy that should be closed between a current or projected actuality and a necessary or highly desirable end result (unmet need)—as judged by a relevant person or group using multiple objective criteria that have been agreed upon" (p. 20). This definition is a combination of discrepancy and level of necessity, where the amount of need varies directly with level of necessity and inversely with amount of discrepancy. Therefore, both of the following statements of need are valid according to this definition: "our students' needs for job information and employer contacts are well taken care of by the placement office on this campus," but "they have a serious need for more counseling prior to their interviews with prospective employers." This definition is also congruent with Burton and Merrill's (1977) observation that solutions in cases of unfulfilled (unmet) needs can involve both increased fulfillment and lowered thresholds of desirability or satisfaction.

This definition is pertinent to all the different types of need outlined in the following section. It also pertains whether one is referring to needs of prospective or enrolled students, of the college or one of its programs, of faculty or staff, of the local community or the region, or of society at large or specific groups within society. It also allows persons to speak in terms of past tense, current tense, or future tense when talking about needs—former needs, current needs, or projected needs.

According to this definition, it is proper to use self-report of wants as an indicator of need, but the self-report must have been gathered in an objective, unbiased manner, and there must also be other supporting evidence. Multiple sources of evidence, or multiple criteria as this is called in the definition, will normally lead to increased assurance of actual need (increased reliability and validity) if objectivity is of paramount concern when gathering each type of evidence.

This definition still has a potential problem of not specifying when the necessity or desirability becomes significant enough to be classified a need, or when the discrepancy between fulfillment and unfulfillment becomes significant enough to warrant that an unmet need has been created. This is necessary, however, if it is to be generic in nature and apply to all the types of need that have been identified. Nevertheless, the definition does indicate that this is properly determined by the judgment of a relevant person or group (identification as a relevant person or group depends upon the situation) using multiple, objective, agreed-upon criteria (the arbiters of the criteria are not specified, but once again it varies with the situation).

Characterizing Needs

If one is trying to identify and assess needs, it is important to be very clear about whose needs are of concern. The tendency of needs assessors has been to not be specific enough about whose needs are being identified and analyzed, and to not consider separately the needs of specific subgroups. Similarly, needs assessors too often do not delineate ahead of time which specific types of needs are of concern to them.

Whose Needs Are of Concern? As mentioned earlier, the focus of a needs-assessment study can be on needs within the institution (for example, courses, programs, departments, enrolled students, faculty, or administrators) or outside the institutions (for example, prospective students, the local citizenry, or groups or organizations within the local community, such as employers). It is important to delineate at the earliest stages of the study exactly whose needs are of concern (where "whose" might even include such entities as organizations and the ecological environment).

A comprehensive, two-level classification of groups and entities for which someone in postsecondary eduation might want to assess needs was developed as a part of the National Center for Higher Education Management Systems (NCHEMS) Outcomes Structure (Lenning and others, 1977). It is presented in Figure 1. The focus there was on *audiences,* the persons, groups, or other entities that could potentially receive or be affected by postsecondary education outcomes. Various needs assessments have been conducted with many of these groups and communities.

The information in Figure 1 is not sufficiently detailed to effectively tailor program activities to the characteristics and situation of the audience, or to those of many outcome studies at the program level. The reason additional levels of detail are not included is that any further subdivisions could be based on several equally valid factors, and while one user of the Structure might want one breakdown, another person with a different philosophy, problem, and context might want a second breakdown. For example, students within a program could be usefully subdivided into: (1) those majoring in the program versus those only taking courses in the program, (2) age groupings, (3) commuter students versus resident students, (4) underclassmen versus upperclassmen, (5) groupings according to disadvantaged status, (6) men and women, (7) groupings according to life and career goals or aspiration levels, and so forth. Rather than provide alternative formal breakdowns of each second-level category shown, the decision was made to provide procedures for users of the Structure to develop their own more detailed breakdowns tailored to their specific problem, conern, or other need context (Lenning, 1977a). Such more detailed categories of groups are necessary for needs assessment studies related to program planning. In planning a curricular program for students, it is important to consider the special needs of important student subgroups.

An additional word should be said about the needs of groups, organizations, and communities as compared to the needs of individuals. Many people have assumed that the needs of a group are merely aggregations of the needs of individuals within that group. It is true

Figure 1. Categories of Persons, Groups, and Other Entities of Possible Concern in Assessments of Needs

10. **Individual/Group Clients**—This category refers to persons or groups of persons who are direct clients of the postsecondary education unit of concern and/or their immediate associates, such as family and relatives or peers.
    11. *Students*—Individuals or groups of individuals who currently are enrolled in the program, institution, or system of postsecondary education.
    12. *Former Students*—Individuals or groups of individuals who formerly were enrolled in the program, institution, or system of postsecondary education.
    13. *Family and Relatives of Students or Former Students*
    14. *Peers and Associates of Students or Former Students*
    15. *Faculty*
    16. *Staff Other than Faculty*
    17. *Other Individual/Group Clients*—An example would be an individual who is none of the above but is served by an advisory service offered by the college.
20. **Interest-Based Communities**—This category refers to large groups that are identified as entities working toward a *well-defined interest or mission.*
    21. *Private Enterprise Communities*—Communities where a major purpose is financial remuneration and profit—for example, corporations, small businesses, and farmers.
    22. *Association Communities*—Communities where members belong on the basis of affiliation rather than employment, such as unions and professional societies.
    23. *Government Communities*—Communities designed to administer government regulations and services, such as city hall, state department of education, and legislative communities.
    24. *Nongovernmental/Public Service Communities Other than the Institution Producing the Outcome*— Nonprofit service organizations, such as schools, hospitals, welfare agencies, philanthropic foundations, colleges (other than the college producing the outcome), and research organizations.
    25. *Institution or Institutional Unit Producing the Outcome*—The postsecondary education institution and/or units within that institution that are perceived as the producer/facilitator of the outcome(s) of concern.
    26. *Other Interest-Based Communities*—An example would be an ad hoc coalition task force of representatives from two or more of the above areas.
30. **Geographic-Based Communities**—This category refers to large groups defined on the basis of *functional territorial boundaries.*
    31. *Local Community*—A township, city, county, metropolitan area, or other type of locality having particular boundaries. It is not necessarily restricted to the legal or jurisdictional boundary, but the functional one in which the impact of the institution is (or should be) directly and physically felt. The boundaries will vary with the institution/program and outcome of concern.
    32. *The State*
    33. *A Region*—An aggregation of states or parts of states.
    34. *The Nation*
    35. *An International Community*
    36. *Other Geographic-Based Communities*—An example would be a research discovery that affects primarily people living in the coldest latitudes, or where it snows heavily.
40. **Aggregates of People**—This category refers to subpopulations of people *distinguished by particular characteristics that may indicate common concerns, needs, or wants,* but who do not necessarily have a common interest or mission, and therefore do not constitute communities.
    41. *Ability Level Subpopulations*—Subpopulations defined according to level of ability/proficiency on general intellectual functioning or specific skills—for example, gifted, typical, disadvantaged, or skilled, semi-skilled, unskilled.
    42. *Age Subpopulations*
    43. *Educational Level Subpopulations*
    44. *Income Level Subpopulations*
    45. *Occupation Subpopulations*
    46. *Physical Disability Subpopulations*
    47. *Race Subpopulations*
    48. *Sex Subpopulations*
    49. *Other Such Aggregates*
50. **Other Audiences**—Examples would be the natural environment that is affected by university-sponsored research (which in turn would be expected to have impacts on audiences such as individuals and communities) and populations of animals (such as the animals affected by efforts to keep depleted species from becoming extinct or by the development of veterinary medicines.

Note: Reprinted from Lenning and others (1977, p. 24), where the focus was on audiences—individuals, groups, communities, organizations, and so on—receiving or being affected by particular outcomes of concern.

that some community and class needs are aggregations of individual needs. For example, an aggregate need exists when more than half of the freshmen entering a college have reading problems. What might have been an individual problem has become a community problem calling for administrative action. There are group needs that are not aggregate needs, however. These tend to be organizational in nature, relating to the effective functioning of the group as a body and to survival and growth of the group. It is even probably that in particular cases some of these group needs will conflict with certain aggregations of individual needs.

Use of the taxonomy in Figure 1 and subdivision of groups through applying important factors such as those listed will undoubtedly produce many more groups than a program can be expected to focus on effectively. Thus, groups with high priority needs should be selected through in-depth discussion and application of criteria agreed upon by the planning team. The criteria appropriate depend on the local situation and context, but could include ones such as the following: How well do we understand the group? How critical are the needs this program could hope to meet? How accessible is the group to us? How much experience do we have in serving this group in other programs? Will the strengths of this program be congruent with the characteristics and needs of the group? What proportion of those desiring to enter the program are expected to be members of this group?

What Types of Needs Are of Concern? Before beginning a needs assessment study, and after determining whose needs are of concern, it is important to specify the types of needs with which the study will concern itself. So that the boundaries of focus are clearly delineated, this should be done along several dimensions as discussed later in this section.

Most needs assessments at the elementary and secondary education level have focused on the needs for particular *educational* outcomes. Needs for outcomes are important in postsecondary education also, and there are many potentially important ones. Lenning (1977b) reviewed the literature for categorizations of outcomes and found eighty-nine of them, some focusing on outcomes for individuals, some on outcomes for society, and some for both. Based on that review and other work, a comprehensive taxonomy of postsecondary education outcomes subject to potential or possible need was developed as shown in Figure 2 (Lenning, 1977a; Lenning and others, 1977). It can be used in planning and developing items for a survey questionnaire designed to gather information about program needs. Definitions and examples of each outcome type are given in both of the NCHEMS documents.

Needs for particular outcomes imply needs for process activi-

Taxonomy of Outcome Types Interpretable in Terms of Needs

Category Code Number	Entity Being Maintained or Changed
1000	**ECONOMIC OUTCOMES**
1100	Economic Access and Independence Outcomes
1110	Economic Access
1120	Economic Flexibility, Adaptability, and Security
1130	Income and Standard of Living
1200	Economic Resources and Costs
1210	Economic Costs and Efficiency
1220	Economic Resources (including employees)
1300	Economic Production
1310	Economic Productivity and Production
1320	Economic Services Provided
1400	Other Economic Outcomes
2000	**HUMAN CHARACTERISTIC OUTCOMES**
2100	Aspirations
2110	Desires, Aims, and Goals
2120	Dislikes, Likes, and Interests
2130	Motivation or Drive Level
2140	Other Aspirational Outcomes
2200	Competence and Skills
2210	Academic Skills
2220	Citizenship and Family Membership Skills
2230	Creativity Skills
2240	Expression and Communication Skills
2250	Intellectual Skills
2260	Interpersonal, Leadership, and Organizational Skills
2270	Occupational and Employability Skills
2280	Physical and Motor Skills
2290	Other Skill Outcomes
2300	Morale, Satisfaction, and Affective Characteristics
2310	Attitudes and Values
2320	Beliefs, Commitments, and Philosophy of Life
2330	Feelings and Emotions
2340	Mores, Customs, and Standards of Conduct
2350	Other Affective Outcomes
2400	Perceptual Characteristics
2410	Perceptual Awareness and Sensitivity
2420	Perception of Self
2430	Perception of Others
2440	Perception of Things
2450	Other Perceptual Outcomes
2500	Personality and Personal Coping Characteristics
2510	Adventurousness and Initiative
2520	Autonomy and Independence
2530	Dependability and Responsibility
2540	Dogmatic/Open-Minded, Authoritarian/Democratic
2550	Flexibility and Adaptability
2560	Habits
2570	Psychological Functioning
2580	Tolerance and Persistence
2590	Other Personality and Personal Coping Outcomes
2600	Physical and Physiological Characteristics
2610	Physical Fitness and Traits
2620	Physiological Health
2630	Other Physical or Physiological Outcomes
2700	Status, Recognition, and Certification
2710	Completion or Achievement Award
2720	Credit Recognition
2730	Image, Reputation, or Status
2740	Licensing and Certification
2750	Obtaining a Job or Admission to a Follow-up Program

Category Code Number	Entity Being Maintained or Changed
2000	**HUMAN CHARACTERISTIC OUTCOMES (continued)**
2760	Power and/or Authority
2770	Job, School, or Life Success
2780	Other Status, Recognition, and Certification Outcomes
2800	Social Activities and Roles
2810	Adjustment to Retirement
2820	Affiliations
2830	Avocational and Social Activities and Roles
2840	Career and Vocational Activities and Roles
2850	Citizenship Activities and Roles
2860	Family Activities and Roles
2870	Friendships and Relationships
2880	Other Activity and Role Outcomes
2900	Other Human Characteristic Outcomes
3000	**KNOWLEDGE, TECHNOLOGY, AND ART FORM OUTCOMES**
3100	General Knowledge and Understanding
3110	Knowledge and Understanding of General Facts and Terminology
3120	Knowledge and Understanding of General Processes
3130	Knowledge and Understanding of General Theory
3140	Other General Knowledge and Understanding
3200	Specialized Knowledge and Understanding
3210	Knowledge and Understanding of Specialized Facts and Terminology
3220	Knowledge and Understanding of Specialized Processes
3230	Knowledge and Understanding of Specialized Theory
3240	Other Specialized Knowledge and Understanding
3300	Research and Scholarship
3310	Research and Scholarship Knowledge and Understanding
3320	Research and Scholarship Products
3400	Art Forms and Works
3410	Architecture
3420	Dance
3430	Debate and Oratory
3440	Drama
3450	Literature and Writing
3460	Music
3470	Painting, Drawing, and Photography
3480	Sculpture
3490	Other Fine Arts
3500	Other Knowledge, Technology, and Art Form Outcomes
4000	**RESOURCE AND SERVICE PROVISION OUTCOMES**
4100	Provision of Facilities and Events
4110	Provision of Facilities
4120	Provision or Sponsorship of Events
4200	Provision of Direct Services
4210	Teaching
4220	Advisory and Analytic Assistance
4230	Treatment, Care, and Referral Services
4240	Provision of Other Services
4300	Other Resource and Service Provision Outcomes
5000	**OTHER MAINTENANCE AND CHANGE OUTCOMES**
5100	Aesthetic-Cultural Activities, Traditions, and Conditions
5200	Organizational Format, Activity, and Operation
5300	Other Maintenance and Change

Note: Reprinted from Lenning and others (197, p. 27).

ties. For example, student outcome needs may suggest a need for special methodologies, classroom environments, faculty-student ratios, teaching strategies, instructor characteristics, innovative techniques, and so on. One can also focus usefully on such process needs directly, not merely inferring them from outcome needs. In addition, there are needs in postsecondary education less directly related to outcomes, such as needs for financial aid for program students, needs for information about programs, and needs for making program use of campus housing facilities.

When assessing needs, the focus can be general and diffused (wide-band study) or it can be specific and detailed (narrow-band study). A wide-band study will be concerned with broad categories of needs while a narrow-band study will be concerned with specialized and detailed need categorizations. Lenning and others (1979) have identified a number of systems for classifying needs, some of them broad-band in focus (for example, Maslow's, 1968, need hierarchy, Parson's, 1950, community need categories, and Bradshaw's Taxonomy of Social Need, 1972) while others have a narrow-band focus (for example, Murray's, 1938, categories of manifest and latent needs, Kinnick's, 1975, Taxonomy of Information Needs of Prospective Students, and the Mooney Problem Checklist scales, Pagels, 1973).

A broad-band focus can cover the entire array of possible student need and quickly and efficiently identify problem areas or the areas where the most unmet need is present. Then, for the areas identified as critical need areas, a narrow-band focus can be used to get a specific, in-depth picture of the specific needs present and their context. For example, a broad-band study may identify (1) program information needed by prospective students, (2) needs for self-concept growth, and (3) need for counseling as three critical need areas. Then, narrow-band study can be used as a follow-up to identify for these three areas: (1) specifically which needed program information is not being provided or is being provided in an inadequate manner, (2) where the self-concept is lacking and not lacking for most students entering the program, and (3) what the specific advising needs of students are.

Many of the categorizations of needs that have been developed place needs into categories along a continuum in a particular dimension. Examples of such bipolar dimensions are: developmental tasks of early life versus developmental tasks of old age, basic versus learned (or derived) needs, personal versus social problems resulting in needs, maintenance versus incremental needs, conscious versus unconscious needs, general versus specific needs, current versus projected needs, critical versus routine needs, instructional versus support needs, economic versus noneconomic needs, needs for goods or products versus needs for services, easy-to-measure needs versus difficult-to-measure needs, and short-term or short-duration needs versus long-term or long-duration needs. Thinking in terms of such dimensions can be helpful for determining and setting the appropriate and desired boundaries of focus in planning for an assessment of needs. Thinking in such terms can also help those responsible for needs assessment to focus their priorities within these boundaries. No program can hope to meet all identified needs, and priorities must be developed based on logical criteria of which needs should be accorded major, minor, or no focus within the program.

Assessing Needs

As has been discussed, one must specifically determine whose needs and what types of needs, for each group, are to be assessed before plans are begun for conducting a needs assessment study. Now some important considerations relating to the conduct of the assessment itself will be discussed, briefly.

Collecting valid and reliable evidence of need or needs is a necessary and crucial part of every needs-assessment study. For any met and unmet need, a number of relevant indicators and measures usually apply. Generally, some will be better indicators of the presence of the need than others, and such factors as whose needs are being assessed can affect the validity of the indicator or measure. (For example, a test designed for and normed on eighteen- to twenty-year-old college students may not be a valid measure for older students.) Therefore, multiple indicators and measures should be used whenever feasible. Increased assurance of validity (that it is a real need) is achieved if they all indicate the same thing about a need, and in addition, tailoring the data collection system to different groups is facilitated by multiple indicators. When one measure is less valid and reliable, another measure may be more valid and reliable.

Currently, most needs surveys are administered solely to the client groups whose needs are being assessed. It is important not to ignore client self-reports about their perceived needs, but other data can be used as well. Implications about need can be derived from client reports about such things as school environment, peers, disappointments or dissatisfactions, successes and achievements, activities, problems, and complaints. Baird (1976), for example, discusses the importance of identifying and remedying "brass tacks." Surveys can also be usefully administered to relevant others for their observations and judgments. Relevant others for students include those who work with them and/or have special concerns about them, such as counselors, advisors, instructors, institutional and program administrators, parents, and student peers. Such relevant others can perhaps be more objective than the student whose needs are being assessed, and many of these other groups clearly have more experience and expertise in making such judgments. Profiles showing how different groups view the situation can be quite revealing, and the pattern of similarities and discrepancies may significantly facilitate understanding of needs.

When outcome needs are of concern, performance measures and history (trends) become very important, but self- and other-report data are still desirable as supplemental indicators. Other useful supplemental data include frequency counts from institutional records concerning such things as attendance, complaints, amount of use (and ratings) of tutorial services, requests received for assistance of various kinds, and so forth. Similarly, statistics from governmental and other community agencies can provide useful supplemental evidence for studies of community needs for curricular programs. What others have found in similar types of institutions, programs, and locales can also be useful supplemental evidence if care is taken to examine closely how the other situations were similar and exactly how they were different from the one of concern. In regard to the various types of data that have already been collected (some have termed these *secondary data*), it should be noted that although they save costs and time in addition to providing useful supplemental evidence, they can lead to problems if great care is not taken in their use. Boyd and Westfall (1972) provide criteria for determining when particular secondary data are acceptable for a particular situation and use, and they also discuss precautions that can help one avoid the potential pitfalls.

Concerning data collection methods, what will work for one group may not work for another. For example, there are special problems in reaching and getting useful and valid data from prospective students and the community that are not present for enrolled students; and within each group there are subgroups that could provide challenges (for example, low-income minorities) to keep unintended biases from occurring. Needs assessors generally limit themselves to several types of traditional instruments: questionnaires, paper-and-pencil tests, and interviews. However, other methods may be just as reliable and valid for the situation at hand and should be considered as alternatives and supplements to the traditional instruments. Lenning (1978) came across fifty different methods in the literature that were found valid and useful in certain situations for assessments of various kinds, including needs assessments. (Examples include the following: charettes, buzz groups, speak-ups, in-basket techniques, role playing and other simulations, open-ended interviews, task analysis and critical incident techniques.) Yet most needs assessors never even consider such nontraditional methods shown to be practical, valid, reliable, and cost efficient for particular purposes and contexts. As with indicators and measures, and for the same reasons, the use of multiple data collection methods is desirable—and the large variety of data collection methods available can facilitate this.

Interpretation and use of needs data are also crucial elements in a needs assessment study, and too often the application of needs assessment results is ineffective. If needs data are going to have practical impact, the users of the needs assessment results (whether instructors, curriculum developers, program administrator, or program support staff) must be precisely identified early in the assessment planning process, prior to conducting the study. Input should be solicited from them concerning their specific concern, what needs information will be helpful to them in their planning decisions, and in what format they would like to see the results. Once analyses are completed, brief, concise reports tailored to each person's information needs should be sent to them. Additional ways to increase the impact of the results are also available (Lenning and others, 1979).

A number of needs assessment models have been developed for use in the educational setting. Most, but not all, have been discrepancy based. Those developed at the elementary and secondary educational levels have tended to be general in their focus. Thus some of the concepts and procedures they discuss may be useful also at the postsecondary level (for example: Coffing and Hutchinson, 1974; English and Kaufman, 1975; Hoepfner and others, 1972; Klein and others, 1971; Lewis, 1973; Morgan, 1975; New Jersey State Department of Education, 1974; Read, 1974; and the various other models reviewed by Adams, 1976, Kaufman, 1972, and Witkin, 1975, 1976). Conversely, postsecondary education models have tended to be more diverse and specific in their focus: vocational, occupational, and continuing education needs (Adams, 1976; Brown, 1974; Keim and others, 1975; Putnam, 1970; Smith, 1968; Tucker, 1973); environmental needs (Aulepp and Delworth, 1976); course-level needs (Burton and Merril, 1977); community needs (Central Florida Community Colleges Consortium, 1973; Gollattscheck and others, 1976; League of California Cities, 1975; Selgas, 1977); needs of the handicapped student (Coffing, Hodson, and Hutchinson, 1973); community information and service needs (Gotsick, 1974); overall curricular needs (Gray, 1974; Hamilton, 1973; Pagels, 1974); administrative functioning needs (Higher Education Management Institute, 1977); prospective students' needs for institutional and program information (Kinnick and Lenning, 1976; Lenning and Cooper, 1978); state-level needs for career education

(McCaslin and Lave, 1976); needs related to performance problems (Mager and Pipe, 1970); goal needs (Peterson, 1976); curricular needs in programs for emergency ambulance personnel (Shook, 1969); and student financial aid needs (the models developed by ACT and CSS). Diverse and specialized models such as many of those above demonstrate the importance of tailoring concepts and procedures to the uniqueness of the conditions and situation. For example, an assessment of the curricular needs in a program for emergency ambulance personnel has to be quite different from one assessing curricular needs in a fine arts program, even though they are both focusing on curricular needs and are both using a critical incident technique.

Many needs assessment studies only try to identify needs. Yet, more is needed (Beatty, 1976): (1) a ranking of needs according to how critical they are and (2) information that can help one to understand why the need occurred and how to best meet it. In addition to not attempting to perform the latter function, almost all of the available needs assessment models, even though they may rank the needs, make use of overly simple and ineffective decision rules that do not consider enough factors or consider each factor in isolation from the others. (Here is where profile analysis—referred to earlier in this section—becomes especially important.) Another problem with many of the models is their tendency to key completely on the current situation without projecting into the future, making the results of such assessments less useful than they might be for evaluating goals, for modifying or reformulating goals, or for developing new goals to meet changing conditions. For example, suppose that there is a trend (based on data over the last three years) toward continually increased severity of communication skills deficiency for incoming students. If the program planner focuses only on the current level of skill deficiency for students entering the program, the planning would probably be less effective than if the trend were also noted and carefully considered. Lenning and others (1979) explore these problems in detail and discuss some possible solutions. They also provide in-depth and extended discussion about all of the other topics covered in this chapter.

Needs assessment clearly is a viable tool to assist administrators and faculty members concerned about meeting client and community needs for programs. Progress in the development of this area must take place, however, before it can begin to reach its full potential.

References

Adams, K. A. "National Large Cities Vocational Education Needs Study." Unpublished doctoral dissertation, Ohio State University, 1976. (Published as a research report under the same title by the Center for Vocational Education, Ohio State University, Columbus, Ohio.)

Aulepp, L., and Delworth, E. *Training Manual for An Ecosystem Model: Assisting and Designing Campus Environments.* Boulder, Colo.: Western Interstate Commission for Higher Education, 1976.

Baird, L. L. "Structuring the Environment to Improve Outcomes." In O. T. Lenning (Ed.), *New Directions for Higher Education: Improving Educational Outcomes,* no. 16. San Francisco: Jossey-Bass, 1976.

Baumheier, E. C., and Heller, G. A. *Analysis and Synthesis of Needs Assessment Research in the Field of Human Services.* Denver: Center for Social Research and Development, University of Denver, 1974.

Beatty, P. T. "A Process Model for the Development of an Information Base for Community Needs Assessment: A Guide for Practitioners." Paper presented at annual meeting of the Adult Education Research Conference, Toronto, 1976. (ED 128 616)

Boyd, H. W., and Westfall, R. *Marketing Research. (3rd ed.) Homewood, Ill.: Irwin, 1972.*

Bradshaw, J. "The Concept of Social Need." *New Society,* 1972, *19,* 640–643.

Brown, B. W. *Methods of Needs Assessment Used in Continuing Education Program Development at Two-Year Colleges in the State of New York.* 1974. (ED 103 610)

Burton, J. K., and Merrill, P. F. "Needs Assessment: Goals, Needs, and Priorities." Lincoln, Nebr.: University of Mid-America, 1977.

Central Florida Community Colleges Consortium. *Educational Needs Assessment: A Simulation Model for Humanistic Planning.* Gainesville: Center for Community Assessment, University of Florida, 1973. (ED 099 025)

Coffing, R. T., Hodson, W. A., and Hutchinson, T. E. *A Needs Analysis Methodology for Education of the Handicapped, Final Report of Comm. Program No. 85-404.* New Haven, Conn.: Area Cooperative Eduational Services, 1973.

Coffing, R. T., and Hutchinson, T. E. "Needs Analysis Methodology: A Prescriptive Set of Rules and Procedures for Identifying, Defining, and Measuring Needs." Paper presented at annual convention of the American Educational Research Association, Chicago, 1974. (ED 095 654)

English, F. W., and Kaufman, R. A. *Needs Assessment: A Focus for Curriculum Development.* Washington, D.C.: Association for Supervision and Curriculum Development, 1975. (ED 107 619).

Gollattscheck, J., and others. *College Leadership for Community Renewal: Beyond Community-Based Education.* San Francisco: Jossey-Bass, 1976.

Gotsick, P. *Community Survey Guide for Assessment of Community Information and Service Needs.* Public Library Training Institutes Library Service Guide No. 2. Morehead: Kentucky Appalachian Adult Education Center, Morehead State University, 1974. (ED 087 392)

Gray, R. W. "Need Assessment Strategy in the Process of Educational Planning." Unpublished doctoral dissertation, University of Pittsburgh, 1973.

Hamilton, D. L. *A Survey of Educational Needs: Secondary School and Community College.* Columbus, Ohio: Battelle Center for Improved Education, 1972, 1973.

Higher Education Management Institute. *Needs Assessment and Planning: Managers Handbook.* (Preliminary ed.) Coconut Grove, Fla.: Higher Education Management Institute, 1977.

Hoepfner, R., and others. *A Guidebook for CSE/Elementary School Evaluation Kit: Needs Assessment.* Boston: Allyn & Bacon, 1972.

Kaufman, R. A. *Educational System Planning.* Englewood Cliffs, N.J.: Prentice-Hall, 1972.

Keim, W. A., and others. *A Manual for Establishing a Community College Community Services Program: A Practical Guide to the Community Based Performance Oriented Institution of Postsecondary Education.* Blackburg: Virginia Polytechnic and State University, 1975. (ED 110 139).

Kinnick, M. K. "Information for Prospective Students About Postsecondary Education: A Partial Assessment of Need." Unpublished doctoral dissertation, University of Colorado at Boulder, 1975.

Kinnick, M. K., and Lenning, O. T. "The Information Needs of Prospective Students." Unpublished resource paper, National Task Force on Better Information for Student Choice, 1976. (Available from the National Center for Higher Education Management Systems, Boulder, Colo.)

Klein, S. P., and others. *Procedures for Needs-Assessment Evaluation: A Symposium.* CSE Report No. 67. Los Angeles: Center for the Study of Evaluation, UCLA Graduate School of Education, 1971. (ED 055 111)

League of California Cities. *Assuming Human Needs.* Sacramento: League of California Cities, 1975.

Lenning, O. T. *The Outcomes Structure: An Overview and Procedures for Applying It in Postsecondary Education Institutions.* Boulder, Colo.: National Center for Higher Education Management Systems, 1977a.

Lenning, O. T. *Previous Attempts to Structure Educational Outcomes and Outcome-Related Concepts: A Compilation and Review of the Literature.* Boulder, Colo.: National Center for Higher Education Management Systems, 1977b.

Lenning, O. T. "Assessing Student Educational Progress." *AAHE College and University Bulletin,* 1978, *30* (7), 3-6. (*ERIC/Higher Education Research Currents,* 1978)

Lenning, O. T., and Cooper, E. M. *Guidebook for Colleges and Universities: Presenting Information to Prospective Students.* Boulder, Colo.: National Center for Higher Education Management Systems, 1978.

Lenning, O. T., and others. *A Structure for the Outcomes of Postsecondary Education.* Boulder, Colo.: National Center for Higher Education Management Systems, 1977.

Lenning, O. T., and others. "Identifying and Assessing Needs in Postsecondary Education: A Review and Synthesis of the Literature." Unpublished manuscript. Boulder, Colo.: National Center for Higher Education Management Systems, 1979.

Lewis, J. L. *Needs Assessment Guidelines.* Columbus: Ohio Department of Education, Division of Planning and Evaluation, 1973.

McCaslin, N. L., and Lave, J. *Needs Assessment and Career Education: An Approach for the States.* Columbus, Ohio: Center for Vocational Education, 1976.

Mager, R. R., and Pipe, P. *Analyzing Performance Problems; Or You Really Oughta Wanna.* Belmont, Calif.: Fearon, 1970.

Maslow, A. H. *Toward a Psychology of Being.* (2nd ed.) Princeton, N.J.: Van Nostrand, 1968.

Morgan, J. M. *Conducting Local Needs Assessment: A Guide.* TM Report 44. Princeton, N.J.: ERIC Clearinghouse on Tests, Measurement, and Evaluation, 1975. (ED 117 188)

Murray, H. A. "Proposals for a Theory of Personality." In H. A. Murray, and others (Eds.), *Explorations in Personality: A Clinical and Experimental Study of Fifty Men of College Age.* New York: Oxford University Press, 1938.

New Jersey State Department of Education. *Needs Assessment in Education: A Planning Handbook for School Districts.* Trenton: New Jersey State Department of Education, 1974.

Pagels, C. F. "The Development of a Process for Determining Specific Criteria for a Student Needs Based Curriculum." Unpublished doctoral dissertation, University of Virginia, 1973.

Parsons, T. *The Social System.* New York: Free Press, 1951.

Peterson, R. E., and Uhl, V. P. *Institutional Goals Inventory Manual.* Princeton, N.J.: Educational Testing Service, 1976.

Putnam, C. E. "Development and Application of a Decision-Making Model for Assessing Need for Occupational Education in a Community College." Unpublished doctoral dissertation, University of Missouri, 1970.

Read, B. *ESA Needs Assessment Procedures Manual.* Austin, Tex.: Educational Systems Associates, 1974.

Scriven, J. "Special Feature: Needs Assessment." *Evaluation News, 1977, 1,* 25-28. (Available from Program Development Center, Aymer I. Hamilton Building, California State University-Chico, Chico, California.)

Selgas, J. W. *Community Educational Needs Assessment: The Capital Region of Pennsylvania.* Harrisburg, Pa.: Harrisburg Area Community College, 1977.

Shook, L. L. "Need Analysis: Adult Education Programs for Emergency Ambulance Personnel." Unpublished master's thesis, University of Iowa, 1969.

Smith, H. K. "A Plan for Developing a Program of Adult Education to Meet the Needs of a Local Community." Unpublished doctoral dissertation, Rutgers University, 1968. (ED 037 600)

Taylor, E. N., and others. *Procedures for Surveying School Problems: Some Individual, Group, and System Indicators.* Alexandria, Va.: Human Resources Research Organization, 1974. (ED 106 375)

Tucker, K. D. "Educational Needs Assessment, A Simulation Model for Humanistic Planning." Paper presented at the annual convention of the Association of Educational Data Systems, New Orleans, April 1973. (ED 087 413)

Witkin, B. R. "Needs Assessment Models: A Critical Analysis." Paper presented at annual conventin of the American Educational Research Association, San Francisco, 1976.

Witkin, B. R. *An Analysis of Needs Assessment Techniques for Educational Planning at State, Intermediate, and District Levels.* Hayward, Calif.: Office of the Alameda County Superintendent of Schools, 1975. (ED 108 370)

Oscar T. Lenning, senior associate at the National Center for Higher Education Management Systems (NCHEMS), joined the NCHEMS staff in 1974 after serving eight years on the research staff of the American College Testing Program. He has also served as a college counselor, student activities director, memorial union night manager, and secondary school teacher. His research and publications have dealt primarily with students, college outcomes, and goals, prediction, evaluation, needs assessment, data collection and application, and planning and communication.

*A case history that recounts the evolutionary development of a
unified evaluation, budgeting, and planning system at
Michigan State University over a period of eight years—
a system that is strongly based upon the collection
and analysis of department, college, and
institutional data.*

Using Institutional Data to Plan Academic Programs—A Case History

Thomas M. Freeman
William A. Simpson

Although practitioners in business and operations research have come to realize the value of insights gained from the narration of specific case histories, few if any books and articles on planning in higher education have adopted this technique. This chapter is a chronological narrative that describes the development of a planning, evaluation, and budgeting process used at Michigan State University. The discussion focuses on the evolutionary nature of this development and demonstrates how evaluation and data have come to play such an important role in tying the components of planning and budgeting together. We have felt it essential to provide examples of report formats and schedules, but it is equally important that attention be paid to the economic and attitudinal conditions existing during the various phases, for it was these environmental conditions that largely determined what could be done and what had to be changed.

Background

Michigan State University is a large, public supported, land grant, research-oriented institution—an excellent example of what is now termed a multiversity. With significant components of its budget depending in varying degrees upon the university's relationships with the state legislature and executive branch, the general public, federal and private grant sources, and the agricultural industry, the industry must be responsive to many groups, not all of whom have complementary interests. To fulfill its obligation in instruction, public service, and research during a period of constrained resources obviously requires many difficult allocation decisions. Academic planning provides the thread of continuity that ties these scattered decisions together to make their collective results predictable and effective. The burden of academic planning falls primarily upon the provost, who, as chief academic officer, administers an organization consisting of 102 departments and 96 support units. His principle staff support in this endeavor has been the Office of Institutional Research which, as one of the oldest such offices (established in 1959) in the country, has had the time to acquire the personnel and develop the systems necessary to support a data-oriented planning process.

Since 1973 all planning, evaluation, and budgeting for the academic sector has taken place within a process called the Annual Evaluation and Report (AER). From the perspective of the present, it is clear that this process has passed through two distinct evolutionary phases and is currently in transition toward a third. The luxury of a six-year time span in which to gradually develop the AER was indeed fortuitous; under a more stringent timetable we could have repeatedly made the error of applying the right idea at the wrong time. What follows is a narration that traces an evaluation/planning process through a span of six years, relating its inadequacies and modifications to the conditions of the times.

Phase I—Evaluation and Budgeting (1972–1976)

Initial Conditions. By 1972 it was apparent that higher education was entering a period in which the economics of the preceding decade did not apply. However, for a major institution funded primarily by the appropriations of a wealthy state, the economic slowdown did not portend an alarming situation—certainly nothing of crisis proportions. Unit administrators and faculty, accustomed as they were to their roles as academic entrepreneurs, were inclined to read the financial signs with considerably more optimism than warranted. The provost, caught between a forward-looking, independent faculty and the realities of an appropriation cutback, steered a prudent, middle-of-the-road course. The situation clearly called for a wiser distribution of diminishing resources, which in turn called for better management information. Up to this point, unit administrators communicated the accomplishments, activities, and problems of their units to the provost in an annual report. Likewise, they developed their budget requests in a largely unconstrained manner, without regard for the relationship with performance. Such an unstructured and one-sided report, while informative and easy to read, was of little value in making the required allocation decisions. The annual report was scrapped. Although its replacement, the Annual Evaluation and Report (AER), was similar enough in name to comfort the more apprehensive unit administrators, the second word in the title signaled that the AER would be far different from its predecessor.

The Prototype AER. This new report was developed by members of the Office of Institutional Research working closely with the Office of the Provost. Since the university had a particularly well-developed and flexible data base, it was decided to use quantitative data to achieve two necessary ends: to provide the provost with a quantitative assessment of all units by comparing them across an array of common variables and to exert pressure on unit administrators to develop more realistic budgets. The final product was ready for use during fiscal year 1973—1974 and was distributed in the form of three schedules. The schedules A, B, and C were designed for instructional departments, academic support units, and deans, respectively. An AER Schedule A consisted of three pages of data summarizing the department's instruction, research, and public service activities: a page requesting self-assessment of the department, with particular emphasis on implications drawn from the data, and two budgets—an allocation budget for the oncoming fiscal year and an asking budget for the following year. The dean's AER, Schedule C, was nearly identical in form except for its design, which was to assist the dean in assembling the department self-evaluations and budget requests into a comprehensive college evaluation and budget request. Because the support units are considerably different in function, a standardized schedule was impossible. Thus each support unit received a Schedule B containing questions that were specifically designed for it. Also, the absence of instructional outputs significantly reduced the size of the data section. The AER was initiated in February with distribution of the reports and concluded in May with a series of conferences between the provost and his staff and each college dean.

Although this procedure and new report format were far more

demanding of unit administrators, they caused a much milder outcry than expected by those who follow faculty affairs closely. Certainly, some of this softening of public reaction was due to the low-key nature of the unit evaluation requested the first year. A more important factor, however, was the obvious usefulness of the data to unit administrators. At last they had, in a single compact package, information about their unit and how it compared to various college and university averages. These were data that could be used to determine how the department was functioning, to indicate what had to be improved, and, very importantly, to support their budget request.

At the college level, the dean was able to use these data in a comparative manner to establish relative priorities among the budget requests received from his departments and support units.

That the first AER was noticeably weak in planning was, in fact, deliberate. It was felt that, inasmuch as a reasonable, well-supported budget represents a rudimentary form of planning, perhaps that was all we could initially attempt. The mood of the times and the many difficulties associated with gaining acceptance for a new process seemed to dictate a slow start; we later found that this was indeed the correct approach.

Refinements. Having briefly described the embryonic AER, it may be best to continue this discussion of the first phase by outlining the major revisions that took place in the next three years and conclude by presenting the problems and conditions that required the conceptual change which brought us into the second phase.

The first AER cycle was successful. Unit administrators sensed a new management mode, one in which allocation decisions were to be made on hard data in a relatively public manner. Deans found that the possession of data for all their units made it far easier for them to separate the bona fide budget requests from the spurious. The provost was satisfied that the final college budget requests and associated use of resources were markedly improved. Using special summary sheets assembled by institutional research (see Dressel and Simon, 1976, p. 90, for example), he began to gain a feeling for the operation of the academic departments and units, which, in the past, did not evolve from reading the expository annual reports—if, indeed, they were read at all. The hard, comparative data, when combined with the more subjective information obtained throughout the year in hundreds of personal contacts, gave the provost considerable reassurance that the correct decisions were being made for at least the next fiscal year.

As confidence in the AER process grew in subsequent cycles, the evaluation aspect was sharpened. In succeeding AER's, unit administrators were asked to make separate and detailed evaluations of their unit's instruction, research, and public service activities. Alongside these assessments, space was provided for the dean and finally the provost to comment. These comments, drawn from each level and shared with all involved parties, constituted a formal dialogue and tended to keep the evaluations forthright and objective. Statements unsupported by the data were questioned; exaggerated claims were pruned. In a similar manner, pressures were brought to bear on the budgets. All completed AER documents were closely analyzed by the Institutional Research staff before each dean met with the provost. Any item in a unit or college budget request that seemed questionable was noted. For example, a request for funds to hire two additional faculty from a department that exhibited low workloads would be noted for discussion at the dean/provost meeting. In a very short time, it became clear that assessment statements and budget request items must agree with the data or else be supportable with other evidence.

As the data grew in significance relative to the budgetary process, a reverse pressure was exerted by the units on the Office of Institutional Research to improve the accuracy, expand the scope, provide finer breakdowns, and delete useless data elements. This was a healthy influence. Wherever possible, unit data were compared to averages for the college, university, and a group of similar departments. In later years, departmental data was obtained from other peer, state-supported institutions and added to the comparative data. Efforts were made to include data on more than simply the instructional outputs of the department; counting scholarly publications and professional activities of the faculty (see Dressel and Simon, 1976) and recording the amount of sponsored research attracted are examples.

The planning aspect of the AER, as conducted in the form of budget requests for two years, was limited even further when it became clear that the budget request for the second year was largely meaningless; these second year budgets were typical results of simply going through the motions of planning without the proper motivation or information. "How," we were repeatedly asked, "do I make up a budget when I don't have any idea of what funding I'll get in the succeeding year?" Because the provost was unwilling to make any commitments concerning future allocations, this question was unanswerable. For the remainder of the first phase, the task of planning budgets two years in advance was dropped and the AER focused on developing the best possible allocation process for the next fiscal year only.

The reluctance on the part of the provost to commit future funds was understandable. During this period the state was undergoing severe economic fluctuations which made higher education appropriations problematic. It was not possible to count on the funds once they were formally appropriated, and on one occasion the university had to carry out a multimillion dollar reduction in midyear. These new uncertainties prompted yet another AER innovation—the idea of preparing dual plans for the possibilities of budget growth or budget reduction. Every unit was directed to develop both a *change plan,* which was growth oriented, and a *flexibility plan,* a euphemism for a budget reduction plan. The change and flexibility plans consisted of incremental budgetary increases and decreases respectively, expressed as operational objectives with associated dollar amounts and listed in order of priority. Armed with a priority-ranked, incremental budget reduction and budget growth plans, the provost stood ready to allocate budget increases and decreases in any degree dictated by the size of the state appropriation. Needless to say, the submittal of two budget requests, each taking the unit in an opposite direction, was not conducive to even short-range planning, but events did not allow otherwise. By the end of the first phase, the need for a more structured planning process at the unit level was becoming obvious. Toward this purpose unit administrators were asked to list their unit goals and relate how they were planning to achieve them.

The reader interested in viewing an abbreviated example of an AER package as it existed at this point is referred to Dressel and Simon (1976).

Problems. The first phase AER had met and in some ways exceeded the purposes for which it was designed. There was no doubt, at any level, that the budgeting process had become more open, focused, and fairer now that comparative data had assumed a lead role. There was a better exchange of information at all levels, which led to better understanding and a better end product—a more effective allocation of scarce resources.

Revisions had been made to adapt the process to changing needs, but by the end of the 1975-1976 fiscal year the consensus was that a major restructuring of both the AER format and some elements of the procedures was necessary. The most pressing problems were: (1) The provost allocated funds to the colleges, not the departments. Often the deans allocated these new resources in a manner that contrasted with what the provost had envisioned. (2) The unit goals and plans, as written out in an expository style in the AER, were difficult to relate to the specifics of the budget requests. (3) There was no clearly outlined procedure to monitor progress toward stated goals after the spring meeting between the provost and the dean. (4) The existence of both a growth budget and a reduction (flexibility) budget, and the attending uncertainty, made even short-range planning difficult.

Phase 2—Planning, Evaluation, and Budgeting (1976-1979)

Outline of the Process. Academic units could carry out and adapt to a considerable amount of restructuring of the AER as long as certain hallmarks of the previous AER were left intact. Superficially, the new AER process looked familiar. (A comparison of the documents used in Phase 1, as shown in Dressel and Simon, 1976, pp. 96-106, with those employed in Phase 2, as shown in Figures 2-14, demonstrates the significant changes.) It still involved the A, B, and C schedules, cycled over a February-June schedule (see Figure 1 for flow of events), and culminated in a dean/provost meeting. The primary intent of the new AER (see Figures 2-14) was to elevate the planning function to a status equal to budgeting, with the data base augmented to facilitate this purpose. A secondary goal was to solve the problems listed at the conclusion of the Phase I narrative. The first item in the new AER package

Figure 1. Annual Evaluation Cycle (Phases 1 and 2)

December	Departments → reporting professional accomplishments / reporting of all funds available to the department → OIR → add to computer
December-January	Provost → approval of AER format and contents → OIR → up-date the computer data base; Registrar → fall term data
February-March	OIR → AER schedules / data sheets → deans → departments and units; departments → unit plans & budgets → dean → college plans & budgets → OIR
March-June	OIR → evaluation of units / summary of data → Provost ↔ deans (discussion of evaluation & budget); deans → summary of discussion with Provost → chairman
June-September	OIR → evaluation and analysis of the proposed allocation & next year's asking budget → Provost → Submission of Budget request to the state; OIR → revise AER according to suggestions; Provost → allocation of next year's funds → Deans

consisted of the familiar seven pages of data (see Figures 2-8). These pages contained all the available data reflecting the operation of the department; this data was useful to chairmen, deans, and the provost for purposes of assessing the department and evaluating the reasonableness of their plans for the future.

Under the new process, every unit was expected to have a plan called the *change plan* (see Figure 9). Departments in areas of expanding opportunities, whether expressed by enrollments or sponsored research, were to develop plans that called for additional support. Units in fields that were static or declining were expected to draw their sights down to planning objectives they could largely finance themselves by reallocation of existing funds (see Figure 10). Regardless of the situation, every unit was required to have a change plan; the status quo was deemed inappropriate.

In addition, units with certain selected colleges were required to have a *flexibility plan* (see Figures 11-12), which would indicate in a series of objectives the manner by which the unit could reduce its base budget by a specific amount. To avoid any conflicts between the flexibility plan and change plan in such units, it was required that any funds listed in the flexibility plan as available for retrenchment could not be used as internal reallocations in the change plan. Thus the implementation of a unit's flexibility plan by the provost would not interfere with progress scheduled in the change plan. If the flexibility plan was not used, the funds earmarked for it would be available for nonrecurring uses.

Each of these two plans were to have an accompanying budget — a change plan budget sheet (see Figure 13) requesting additional funds, and a flexibility plan budget sheet showing what funds were available for withdrawal. The budget and the related plans were tied firmly together by assigning a common code to each planning objective and its corresponding entry in the budget.

Two procedural changes were made. First, the provost wrote each dean indicating the probability of additional funds for the next year and selected those colleges from which a flexibility plan was desired. Second, deans were not given carte blanche to dispose of new funds; such funds were allocated toward specific objectives in the dean's college change plan (see Figure 14). In developing the plan, the dean had had complete freedom to assign priorities to each objective, but the provost reserved the privilege of selecting which objectives he preferred to support. A final meeting in late August was scheduled to resolve any conflicts of purpose that might ensue from this procedure.

The only measure of whether a planning process works is to observe some outcomes: do the planned events occur, and are the

Figure 2. Annual Evaluation, Sections 1 through 6

OFFICE OF INSTITUTIONAL RESEARCH
ANNUAL EVALUATION
SCHEDULE A

DEPARTMENT	ENGLISH	ENG			PBES CATEGORY
COLLEGE	COLL ARTS LETTERS	A+L			ARTS HUM + LETTERS

SECTION 2.2 COMPARATIVE STATISTICS

1. GENERAL FUND BUDGET

	DEPARTMENT			BUDGET				1978-9 BUDGET			
	1977-8	1978-9	INC	INCREASE OR DECREASE				PERCENT DISTRIBUTION			
	ACTUAL	BUDGET	0/0	DEPARTMENT	COLL UNIV PBES			DEPT	COL	UNIV	PBES
				$	0/0	0/0	0/0				
SALARY	1183021	1266515	7	77494	7	8	10	8	97	95	90	93
LABOR	1276	1400	10	124	10	13	-1	5	0	0	1	2
SUPPLIES AND SERVICES	34499	35500	3	1001	3	6	8	7	3	4	7	6
EQUIPMENT	0	0	0	0	0	60	-21	-12	0	0	1	0
TOTAL	1218796	1297415	6	78619	6	8	9		100	100	100	100

2. ALL FUNDS BUDGET
TOTAL BUDGET

	$	0/0
GENERAL FUND	1297415	96
COOP EXT	0	0
EXP STA	1000	0
21 ACCTS	46	0
31 ACCTS	50128	4
71 ACCTS	45509	3
FEDERAL	4619	0
OTHER		
CAPITATION		
ALL UNIV RES FUNDS	7645	1
TOTAL FUNDS	1356234	100
SHARED FUNDS	0	0

3. GENERAL FUND STAFF

	DEPARTMENT			COLLEGE			UNIVERSITY		
	FALL 1977	FALL 1978	INC 0/0	FALL 1977	FALL 1978	INC 0/0	FALL 1977	FALL 1978	INC 0/0
FTE FACULTY	47.49	47.59	0	266.97	275.35	3	1768.09	2042.81	16
FTE GRAD ASSISTANT	15.40	17.21	12	107.89	98.54	-8	645.10	655.10	2
FTE TOTAL FACULTY	62.89	64.80	3	374.66	373.89	0	2413.19	2697.91	12
FTE ADMIN-PROF	0.00	0.00	0	1.00	1.00	0	57.29	62.39	9
FTE CLERICAL	5.00	4.00	-19	34.53	32.90	-4	476.45	453.53	-4
FTE TECHNICAL	0.00	0.00	0	1.00	2.00	100	54.72	54.20	0
CONTRIBUTORS	0.00	0.00	0	0.00	0.00	0	1984.00	2254.00	14

4. ALL FUNDS STAFF
BUDGETED RANKED FACULTY

	FTE
GENERAL FUND	38.18
COOP EXT	0.00
EXP STA	0.00
21 ACCTS	0.00
31 ACCTS	0.00
71 ACCTS	0.00
FEDERAL	0.00
OTHER	0.00
CAPITATION	0.00
ALL UNIV RES FUNDS	0.00
TOTAL FUNDS	38.18

5. PROFESSIONAL ACCOMPLISHMENTS - SUMMARIZED

	DEPARTMENTS		COLLEGE		UNIVERSITY	
	CALENDAR YEAR 1977	CALENDAR YEAR 1978				
PUBLISHED OUTPUT/FTRF	118/ 45= 3	95/ 38= 2				
REFEREED PAPERS/FTRF	24/ 45= 1	23/ 38= 1				
BOOKS/FTRF	12/ 45= 0	8/ 38= 0				
DELIVERED PAPERS, RECITALS, SHOWINGS/FTRF	156/ 45= 3	120/ 38= 3				
MAJOR PROFESSIONAL ACCOMPLISHMENTS/FTRF	525/ 45= 12	396/ 38= 10				
ADMINISTRATIVE ACTIVITY/FTRF	142/ 45= 3	135/ 38= 4				
ADVISING DUTIES/FTRF	1055/ 45= 23	932/ 38= 24				
PROPOSALS/FTRF	35/ 45= 1	35/ 38= 1				
EVIDENCES OF MERIT/FTRF	3/ 45= 0	6/ 38= 0				
PATIENT CARE VOLUME/FTRF	0/ 45= 0	0/ 38= 0				

6. CLERICAL RATIOS

	GENERAL FUND FTETF(ACTUAL)/GENERAL FUND CLERICAL(BUDGET)
	DEPARTMENTS COLLEGE UNIVERSITY
FALL 1977	12.58 10.85 5.06
FALL 1978	16.20 11.36 5.95

Comments:

1. The columns labeled 'PBES' contain data averages for a group of departments similar in discipline to the department being evaluated. The label in the upper right corner defines this PBES category.
2. To aid administrators, the computer is programmed to print comments under each data block calling attention to data that is significantly different from the norm. Space limitations did not allow for reproducing such comments.
3. The data in Section 5 are quotients of outputs divided by ranked faculty FTEs. ex:118/45 = 3 is read as 118 published outputs ÷ 45 FTE = 3 outputs per FTE.
4. The column headed "0/0" contains percentages.

Figure 3. Annual Evaluation, Sections 7 and 8

```
DEPARTMENT  ENGLISH               ENG        OFFICE OF INSTITUTIONAL RESEARCH
COLLEGE     COLL ARTS LETTERS     A+L            ANNUAL EVALUATION                        ARTS HUM + LETTERS    PBES CATEGORY
                                                    SCHEDULE A
```

7. TENURE RATIOS

STAFFING FLEXIBILITY (HEADCOUNTS)
ALL FUNDS - BOARD APPOINTMENTS (WITH PAY)

	DEPARTMENT					COLLEGE					UNIVERSITY				
	FALL 1977		FALL 1978			FALL 1977		FALL 1978			FALL 1977		FALL 1978		
	NO.	O/O	NO.	O/O		NO.	O/O	NO.	O/O		NO.	O/O	NO.	O/O	
FULL-TIME															
TENURED FACULTY	38	81	40	74		197	73	201	70		1541	60	1576	59	
TENURE SYSTEM WITHOUT TENURE	7	15	6	11		43	16	42	15		439	17	429	16	
NOT IN TENURE SYSTEM - WITH JOB SECURITY	0	0	0	0		1	0	1	0		17	1	20	1	
- WITHOUT JOB SECURITY	1	2	7	13		22	8	36	13		403	16	500	19	
TOTAL FULL-TIME FACULTY	46	98	53	98		263	98	280	97		2400	94	2525	94	
PART-TIME															
TENURED FACULTY	0	0	0	0		2	1	1	0		7	0	5	0	
TENURE SYSTEM WITHOUT TENURE	0	0	0	0		0	0	0	0		2	0	3	0	
NOT IN TENURE SYSTEM - WITH JOB SECURITY	0	0	0	0		0	0	0	0		1	0	2	0	
- WITHOUT JOB SECURITY	1	2	1	2		4	1	7	2		143	6	152	6	
TOTAL PART-TIME FACULTY	1	2	1	2		6	2	8	3		153	6	162	6	
TOTAL (FULL- AND PART-TIME) FACULTY	47	100	54	100		269	100	288	100		2553	100	2687	100	
FACULTY 60 OR OLDER															
O/O TENURED FACULTY/TENURE SYSTEM	4	9	4	7		26	10	55	19		234	9	340	13	
O/O TENURED FACULTY/TOTAL FACULTY - FULL-TIME		84		87			82		83			78		79	
- TOTAL (FULL- AND PART-TIME)		83		75			75		72			64		62	
O/O TENURED FACULTY + JOB SECURITY/TOTAL FACULTY		81		74			74		70			61		59	
- FULL-TIME		83		75			75		72			65		63	
- TOTAL (FULL- AND PART-TIME)		81		74			74		70			61		60	

8. GENERAL FUND SUPPORT RESOURCES (SUPPORT $ = LABOR + SUPPLIES AND SERVICES + EQUIPMENT)

	SUPPORT $ AS A PERCENTAGE OF SALARY $			SUPPORT CENTS/FALL SCH		
	1976-77	1977-78	1978-79	1976-77	1977-78	1978-79
DEPARTMENT	3	3	5	259	306	321
COLLEGE	4	5	5	449	534	641
UNIVERSITY	12	11	11	1082	1207	1282
PBES	7	7	7	788	883	768
AAU	10	4				

Comments:

1. The staffing of a unit is central to any planning process. The data in Section 7 is used to assess the staffing flexibility of the unit as expressed in terms of temporary faculty, part-time faculty, and faculty approaching retirement age.
2. Many unit administrators requested some comparative data that reflects on the adequacy of supply, labor, and equipment budgets, in order that they can gauge if reductions or increases are reasonable planning options. Section 8 provides this information. The entry labelled 'AAU' represents the aggregation of data collected from twenty-three state-supported institutions belonging to the AAU.

Figure 4. Annual Evaluation, Sections 9 through 12

DEPARTMENT ENGLISH ENG OFFICE OF INSTITUTIONAL RESEARCH PBES CATEGORY
COLLEGE COLL ARTS LETTERS A+L ANNUAL EVALUATION ARTS HUM + LETTERS
SCHEDULE A

9. CLASS HRS/CREDITS AND SCH/FTETF

	DEPARTMENT				COLLEGE				UNIVERSITY				PBES			
	CL H/ CH	CL H/ FTETF	SCH/ FTETF	5 YR AV SCH/FTE	CL H/ CH	CL H/ FTETF	SCH/ FTETF	5 YR AV SCH/FTE	CL H/ CH	CL H/ FTETF	SCH/ FTETF	5 YR AV SCH/FTE	CL H/ CH	CL H/ FTETF	SCH/ FTETF	5 YR AV SCH/FTE
FALL TERMS																
1974	.81	7.76	209.7		.93	9.03	174.2		1.13	9.82	229.1		.91	9.21	205.2	
1975	.91	8.69	195.6		1.15	10.95	172.2		1.43	12.83	233.3		1.07	10.80	203.8	
1976	1.08	10.14	189.1		1.09	9.94	158.9		1.31	11.06	225.1		1.05	9.97	198.3	
1977	1.04	10.54	186.2		1.13	10.40	161.6		1.45	11.69	217.9		1.08	9.77	189.7	
1978-MSU	.93	7.98	177.2	191.3	1.11	9.31	145.5	162.6	1.51	11.56	200.1	220.4	.96	8.84	183.4	195.6
-AAU			214.2													
F.Y.																
1974-5	.81	35.17	803.9		1.06	44.82	673.5		1.10	41.26	822.2		1.00	43.40	776.2	
1975-6	.80	34.43	760.0		1.04	42.99	652.3		1.31	48.74	826.0		1.01	43.25	775.9	
1976-67	1.00	42.67	742.7		1.08	42.94	623.5		1.35	46.94	793.3		1.05	42.11	742.3	
1977-8	.96	40.48	720.6		1.13	43.90	594.6		1.39	46.95	754.5		1.00	39.88	713.4	

10. SCH DISTRIBUTION

STUDENT CREDIT HOURS (SCH)

	DEPARTMENT STUDENT LEVELS					COLLEGE STUDENT LEVELS					UNIVERSITY STUDENT LEVELS				
F.Y. 77-78 COURSE LEVEL	FR-SO	JR-SR	GP	MAS	DR	TOTAL	FR-SO	JR-SR	GP	MAS	DR	TOTAL	FR-SO	JR-SR	GP	MAS	DR	TOTAL
SUB COLLEGE	8	203		58	9	278	361	4125		1338	227	6051	29258	6681	0	1371	235	37545
LOWER DIV	9543	7771		27		17348	46452	41529	45	807	365	89198	557380	261612	546	3149	1121	823808
UPPER DIV	2614	15106		319	93	18132	10545	57756	29	3247	1147	72724	53800	523205	515	24075	5938	607533
UNDER GRAD	12165	23080		404	106	35758	57358	103410	74	5392	1739	167973	640000	791498	1061	28595	7294	1468886
GRAD PROF				0	0	0			0	0	0	24	154	424	48873	696	398	50415
MASTERS	3	147		944	197	1291	28	911	11	5834	1350	8134	8140	356	255	91863	23343	123755
DOCTORS	0	29		260	1032	1321	0	51		524	2250	2825	12	8920	27	5174	31247	36816
GRADUATE	3	176		1204	1229	2612	28	962	11	6358	3600	10959	190	12514	49155	97733	54988	210986
CONTRIBUTED	0			24	6	36		326		120	30	1030	9862		6558	2837	1342	33093
TOTAL	12168	23262		1632	1341	38406	57712	104926	85	11870	5369	179962	650490	812932	56754	129165	63624	1712965

11. WEIGHTED SECTION SIZE OF ORGANIZED CLASSES

	UNDERGRADUATE				GRADUATE			
F.Y.	DEPT	COLL	UNIV	PBES	DEPT	COLL	UNIV	PBES
1973-4	25	25	40	27	14	11	22	11
1974-5	25	25	41	27	15	12	23	12
1975-6	24	25	41	27	14	11	20	11
1976-7	32	25	42	28	13	10	20	11
1977-8	29	23	41	27	10	9	19	9

12. UNWEIGHTED SECTION SIZES F.Y. 1977-78

	UNDERGRADUATE								GRADUATE							
ENROLL	DEPT SEC O/O	COLL SEC O/O	UNIV SEC O/O	PBES SEC O/O	DEPT SEC O/O	COLL SEC O/O	UNIV SEC O/O	PBES SEC O/O
200+	0	0	6	0	36	2	202	2	458	4	63	2	0	0	0	0
101-200	1	3	36	2	125	6	1491	12	275	8	0	0	1	0	26	2	0	0
51-100	13	29	125	8	129	6	1684	13	187	6	0	0	0	0	65	5	0	0
36-50	12	23	37	9	140	6	575	26	4419	35	1281	39	0	0	0	0	80	6	0	0
21-35	14	27	166	40	575	26	4419	35	1281	39	5	0	7	4	238	17	6	4
11-20	13	20	152	36	880	39	3241	26	978	30	3	22	54	27	414	29	47	28
1-10	9	19	22	5	498	22	1050	8	494	15	31	55	138	69	600	42	115	68

Comments:
1. The contact hours per FTE faculty (CL H/FTETF) and SCH/FTETF in Section 9 are two very important workload measures. These data, together with the section size data of Section 11 and 12, constitute our assessment of department workloads.
2. Table 10 was designed to compare the degree of match between course levels and student levels. The deleted computer comments, which point out significant incongruities, greatly facilitate the understanding of this table.

Figure 5. Annual Evaluation, Sections 13 through 17

OFFICE OF INSTITUTIONAL RESEARCH
ANNUAL EVALUATION
SCHEDULE A

DEPARTMENT ENGLISH   ENG
COLLEGE   COLL ARTS LETTERS A+L   ARTS HUM + LETTERS PBES CATEGORY

13. DISTRIBUTION OF ALL-FUNDS FACULTY EFFORT IN FTE

```
                                        DEPT   COLL   UNIV   PBES
                                        FTETF  FTETF  FTETF  FTETF
SPRING 1978
 SCHEDULED INSTRUCTION                   39    169    952    333
 OTHER INSTRUCTION                        1     13    144     34
 ADVISING AND COUNSELING                         8    133     26
 COURSE AND CURRICULUM DEVELOPMENT               3     71     14
 RESEARCH, CREATIVE AND SCHOLARLY ACTIVITY 6    49    658     69
 PROFESSIONAL AND PUBLIC SERVICE-PATIENT CARE    8    105     17
 ADMINISTRATIVE AND COMMITTEE             3     22    205     45
```

14. SCH DISTRIBUTION FALL 1978

```
                              TOTAL    0/0 DISTRIBUTION
                              SCH      DEPT  COLL  UNIV
FACULTY
 ORGANIZED CLASSES            8622      75    75    78
 INDEP-VAR                     333       3     5     6
   TOTAL                      8955      78    80    84

GRAD ASSISTANTS
 ORGANIZED CLASSES            2522      22    20    14
 INDEP-VAR                       3       0     0     1
   TOTAL                      2525      22    20    16

TOTAL                        11480     100   100   100
```

15. SCH TREND

```
            COURSE LEVELS       DEPARTMENT      COLLEGE         UNIVERSITY
                             FALL   F.Y.     FALL   F.Y.      FALL       F.Y.
1974-5 UNDERGRADUATE          92    91       94    93         90         88
       GRADUATE                8     9        6     7         10         12
         TOTAL              12468 42845    69052 218625      534554    1632482

1975-6 UNDERGRADUATE          93    92       94    93         90         89
       GRADUATE                7     8        6     7         10         11
         TOTAL              12236 40922    67134 211463      545994    1670423

1976-7 UNDERGRADUATE          93    92       94    93         90         89
       GRADUATE                7     8        6     7         10         11
         TOTAL              11900 38678    61860 196190      534218    1611634

1977-8 UNDERGRADUATE          95    93       95    94         90         88
       GRADUATE                5     7        5     6         10         12
         TOTAL              11709 38467    60759 187446      536951    1671211
```

16. SELECTED COMPARISONS

```
                                                     STAFF CHANGE
                                                     REQUIRED TO
                                           SCH/FTE   MATCH WORKLOAD
DEPT - FALL AVERAGE                         177
AAU  - AVERAGE                              214      -11 FTE  -16 0/0

DEPT 4 TERM AVERAGE                         721
PBES 4 TERM AVERAGE                         807       -6 FTE  -10 0/0

DEPT 4 TERM AVERAGE WT
 BY COURSE LEVELS                           721
PBES 4 TERM AVERAGE WT
 COURSE LEVELS                              776       -4 FTE   -6 0/0

DEPT - FALL AVERAGE                         177
DEPT - FALL 5 YEAR AVERAGE                  191       -4 FTE   -6 0/0
```

17. SOURCE OF STUDENT ENROLLMENTS

```
          DEPARTMENT COURSES          COLLEGE COURSES
          WITHIN COLL  OTHER COLL     WITHIN COLL  OTHER COLL
F-W-S- 1975-6   5753      6931           27038       30166
F-W-S- 1976-7   5361      6917           24678       27696
F-W-S- 1977-8   4607      7072           22608       27533
```

Comments:
The various SCH/FTE Workload comparisons are translated into terms of staff reductions or additions necessary to equate the workloads under comparison.

Figure 6. Annual Evaluation, Sections 18 through 20

```
DEPARTMENT  ENGLISH            ENG           OFFICE OF INSTITUTIONAL RESEARCH
COLLEGE     COLL ARTS LETTERS  A+L               ANNUAL EVALUATION                    ARTS HUM + LETTERS
                                                     SCHEDULE A                       PBES CATEGORY

18.  CONTACT HOUR DISTRIBUTION FALL-WINTER-SPRING 1977-78     19.  SCH DISTRIBUTION FALL-WINTER-SPRING 1977-78

 TERM      GENERAL FUND    APPOINTMENTS                     TERM      GENERAL FUND    APPOINTMENTS
FREQUENCY     DEPT      COLL UNIV    ALL FUNDS              FREQUENCY     DEPT      COLL UNIV    ALL FUNDS
DISTRIBUTION FTE   O/O  O/O   O/O   DEPT                    DISTRIBUTION FTE   O/O  O/O   O/O   DEPT
                                    FTE   O/O                                                    FTE   O/O
    0        1.92   3   13    21    2.92    4                   0        1.75   3    9    29    1.75    3
  .01- .99   0.00   0    0     1     .33    1                   1-4       .17   0    0     1     .83    1
 1.00-1.99   0.00   0    0     1    0.00    0                   5-14      .10   0    1     2     .76    1
 2.00-3.99  10.00  16    7     7   10.33    7                  15-29     1.00   2    3     5    1.00    2
 4.00-5.99   4.04   6    6     6    4.38    7                  30-49     3.25   5    8     6    3.58    6
 6.00-7.99  11.43  18   15    15   11.43    8                  50-99    12.36  20   18    13   12.69   20
 8.00-9.99   9.38  15   15    15    9.38   12                 100-199   21.76  35   36    19   21.76   33
10.00+      26.23  42   43    39   26.23   32                 200-299   13.67  22   16    14   13.67   21
   TOTAL    63.00 100  100   100   65.00  100                 300-399    5.72   9    5     7    5.72    9
                                                              400+       3.23   5    4    12    3.23    5
                                                                TOTAL   63.01 100  100   100   64.99  100

20.  FALL TERM MAJORS AND ANNUAL DEGREES GRANTED
              DEPARTMENT                               COLLEGE                              UNIVERSITY
         FALL       F.Y.                         FALL       F.Y.                       FALL       F.Y.
        MAJORS    DEGREES                       MAJORS    DEGREES                     MAJORS    DEGREES
BACHELOR
 1973-4   547        211                         2601       686                       24711      6427
 1974-5   532        172                         2592       595                       25853      6313
 1975-6   531        172                         2494       662                       27195      6701
 1976-7   458        139                         2303       581                       26931      6651
 1977-8   444        117                         2126       492                       27599      6672
 1978     393                                    2061                                 27647
MASTER
 1973-4   119         56                          523       204                        4714      2184
 1974-5    99         53                          486       200                        5242      2311
 1975-6    83         33                          451       171                        5346      2504
 1976-7    80         39                          405       143                        4576      2418
 1977-8    70         35                          372       146                        4425      2213
 1978      85                                     373                                  4157
DOCTORAL
 1973-4    81         10                          242        47                        2427       555
 1974-5    85         20                          230        55                        2479       594
 1975-6    77         13                          203        46                        2474       525
 1976-7    78          6                          201        35                        2496       487
 1977-8    67         10                          195        27                        2538       420
 1978      64                                     197                                  2370
SPEC AND PROF
 1973-4     0          0                            0         4                           0        69
 1974-5     0          1                            0         3                           0        63
 1975-6     0          0                            0         2                           0        56
 1976-7     0          0                            0         1                           0        57
 1977-8     0          0                            0         0                           0        46
 1978       0                                       0                                     0
```

Comments:
Sections 18 and 19 were designed to better reveal how workloads are distributed over the faculty. Department averages give no clues to this important consideration.

Figure 7. Annual Evaluation, Section 23

OFFICE OF INSTITUTIONAL RESEARCH
ANNUAL EVALUATION
SCHEDULE A

DEPARTMENT	ENGLISH	ENG
COLLEGE	COLL ARTS LETTERS	A+L

23. RANKING OF DEPARTMENT

ARTS HUM PBES CATEGORY
A+L LETTERS

	DEPT VALUE	UNIV RANK	PBES N RANK	N	MINIMUM	10	20	UNIVERSITY DECILES 30	40	50	60	70	80	90	100

GROUP I (LARGEST VALUE RANKED AS 1)

1. 1976-1977 COMPARISON WITH MICH AVG COST	1.2	42 98	6 6	14	-106.6	-81.9	-47.0	-35.3	-21.1	-11.2	2.7	9.2	19.8	36.7	90.9
2. 1977-1978 COMPARISON WITH MICH AVG COST	21.2	30 99	5 5	15	-101.8	-76.1	-41.5	-20.6	-14.0	-2.8	7.1	21.2	29.7	39.2	89.1
3. O/O CHANGE TO = AAU WORKLOAD SCH/FTE	-17.2	53 81	8 8	16	-61.1	-41.6	-29.4	-19.7	-15.6	-11.0	-3.1	1.0	20.9	35.5	132.1
4. O/O CHANGE TO = WEIGHTED PBES SCH / FTE	-7.0	51 102	5 5	19	-94.7	-58.3	-41.2	-29.8	-19.7	-8.3	1.6	10.4	34.6	55.9	210.1
5. O/O CHANGE TO = UNIV. AVG SCH / FTE	-8.7	41 100	6 6	19	-95.4	-75.3	-63.8	-45.6	-25.9	-15.6	-8.9	2.4	25.7	64.5	221.2
6. O/O CHANGE TO = 5 YR DEPT AVG SCH/FTE	-7.3	41 98	7 7	15	-75.4	-30.2	-22.0	-18.7	-15.1	-9.9	-7.3	-2.3	4.4	8.6	116.6
7. FISCAL YEAR SCH / FTETF	721	42 102	2 2	19	36	191	311	446	586	667	721	804	981	1334	2538
8. FISCAL YEAR CONTACT HOURS/FTETF	40.5	55 102	8 8	19	9.9	23.4	27.9	33.8	39.0	42.2	43.8	48.5	56.0	82.0	224.5
9. UNDER GRAD. COURSE AVERAGE SECTION SIZE	28.6	67 83	4 4	13	8.2	19.7	28.4	32.1	37.0	40.6	44.6	49.8	60.3	77.8	259.2
10. GRADUATE COURSE AVERAGE SECTION SIZE	9.57	57 77	3 3	9	1.00	5.73	8.56	9.91	11.88	13.94	16.44	21.54	24.28	46.61	94.50
11. SCH INCREASE THIS YEAR IN O/O	-.4	52 98	5 5	15	-55.4	-11.8	-7.7	-4.6	-2.3	-.3	3.2	5.6	9.5	16.8	341.9
12. PUBLISHED OUTPUT / ALL-FUNDS FTERF	2.49	60 101	8 8	19	.29	1.13	1.63	2.17	2.47	2.97	3.82	5.89	9.48	13.35	27.37
13. REFEREED PAPERS / ALL-FUNDS FTERF	.60	57 98	3 3	16	.05	.11	.24	.39	.53	.71	1.05	1.27	1.97	3.74	13.57
14. DELIVERED PAPERS / ALL-FUNDS FTERF	3.14	77 102	10 10	19	.05	1.80	2.90	3.49	4.48	5.72	6.78	8.75	11.39	15.81	33.38
15. MAJOR PROF. ACTIVITIES / ALL-FUNDS FTERF	10.4	56 102	9 9	19	.7	3.7	4.9	6.6	9.4	11.5	14.1	18.3	21.9	38.1	104.7
16. ADVISING DUTIES / ALL-FUNDS FTERF	24.4	39 100	8 8	17	.0	2.4	4.2	7.9	11.8	14.1	21.9	27.9	35.4	59.4	169.2
17. 71 ACCT FUNDS / CURRENT GF BUDGET	4	80 94	6 6	13	0	1	6	11	16	21	27	48	67	138	1262
18. 71 ACCT FUNDS / ALL FUNDS FTERF	1313	79 92	6 6	13	20	615	2002	4205	5893	7725	10320	13525	18590	27577	80883
19. O/O TEMPORARY FAC TO TOTAL FULL TIME FAC	13-21	53 90	10 10	17	2.70	5.88	7.84	11.11	13.04	14.89	20.00	26.32	30.00	38.10	80.00
20. FTETF / FTE CLERICAL STAFF	16-20	5 97	2 2	14	1.14	2.11	3.07	3.67	4.54	5.31	6.42	7.34	9.45	12.12	30.95
21. O/O FISCAL YR GRAD. COURSE SCH/TOTAL SCH	6.9	70 100	10 10	18	.0	1.1	3.1	6.0	8.5	9.7	11.5	18.0	52.7	92.2	100.0
22. O/O CHANGE IN SCH/FTE THIS YEAR	-2.9	41 98	5 5	15	-69.1	-30.9	-15.7	-11.1	-8.3	-5.3	-2.8	-1.0	1.8	12.1	175.1
23. OFF CAMPUS SCH ATTRIBUTED TO MSU FAC	1156	8 60	7 7	14	2	12	36	51	79	122	176	277	516	1156	13319
24. NON CREDIT PCEU ATTRIBUTED TO MSU FAC	355	27 67	7 7	13	3	36	63	93	142	227	352	517	1136	1939	14640

GROUP II (SMALLEST VALUE RANKED AS 1)

25. FTETF WITH LESS THAN 200 SCH / FTETF	64.1	36 103	6 6	20	100.0	97.2	89.7	84.4	80.3	72.1	65.7	59.6	54.5	41.6	3.1
26. FTETF WITH LESS THAN 8 CONTACT HRS/FTETF	43.5	46 103	12 12	20	98.1	76.3	62.4	57.5	52.9	48.1	41.4	36.1	31.3	17.0	6.1
27. SUPPORT BUDGET / SALARY BUDGET	2.9	7 104	4 4	19	70.6	25.9	17.6	13.9	11.0	9.2	7.7	6.6	5.1	3.6	1.5
28. SUPPORT CENTS / FALL SCH	321	10 102	5 5	19	118789	8558	4587	2539	2187	1540	1068	761	533	328	60
29. O/O TENURED FAC TO TOTAL FACULTY	74.1	82 102	11 11	19	100.0	82.6	73.8	70.0	64.7	60.0	53.9	48.1	41.7	26.9	11.1

Comments:

This section contains the unit's rank within the university and within a group of similar departments (PBES) as measured across twenty-nine variables. Deans find such a display to be useful in establishing priorities within their college.

Figure 8. 1977-78 Annual Evaluation and Report

OPERATIONAL OBJECTIVE

Report of Progress   unit: Computer Science

Unit Code—Priority	Description	1st year	Comments
C-CPS - 1	To appoint four additional faculty members, in two steps.	$60,000	One new position has been authorized for 1978-79. Recruitment activities now in progress.
C-CPS - 2	To support 10 half-time graduate teaching assistants, in two steps.	19,825 (3,800)	No progress. No new funds made available and not able to shift Labor funds without new resources.
C-CPS - 3	To acquire mini- and microprocessors for student and research laboratories.	20,000	Three minicomputers acquired, with matching fund grant from NSF. University funds supplied to acquire beginnings of microprocessor laboratory.
C-CPS - 4b	To fund previously approved CT-V position.	7,500	$5,000 allocated beginning with 1977-78 budget.
C-CPS - 5	To provide computer terminals for faculty use.	10,000	Two terminals acquired with year-end funds.
C-CPS - 6	To appoint academic advisor.	8,000	No progress.
C-CPS - 7a	To increase availability of self-paced instruction. (1/2 FTE plus two graduate assistants)	19,450	No progress.
C-CPS - 8a	To expand lifelong education program (1/2 FTE)	10,000	No progress.
C-CPS - 9	To provide shortcourses through continuing education.	0	Plans being made for initiation of short courses during 1978.
C-CPS - 10a	To develop graduate project course capabilities. (1/4 FTE)	5,000	No progress.

Comments:
Units use this section, which has a copy of their last year's change plan printed on it, to report what progress has been made toward their stated objectives.

Figure 9. 1977-78 Annual Evaluation and Report
Schedule A: Instructional Units

Unit Change Plan

UNIT CHANGE PLAN

Unit Code–Priority	OPERATIONAL OBJECTIVE Description	FY 78-79	FY 79-80	FY 80-81	FY 81-82	FY 82-83
C-CPS-1	To appoint three additional faculty members, in two steps.	$40,000	60,000	60,000	60,000	60,000
C-CPS-2	To appoint two half-time graduate research assistants (one for Image Processing Laboratory and one for Artificial Language Laboratory).	14,400	14,600	14,600	14,600	14,600
C-CPS-3	To support 10 half-time graduate teaching assistants, in two steps (where undergraduate students are now being utilized).	22,000 (3,800) 25,800	22,000 (3,800) 25,800	41,400 (9,200) 50,600	41,400 (9,200) 50,600	41,400 (9,200) 50,600
C-CPS-4	For undergraduate teaching laboratories, 1) to acquire additional minicomputers and upgrade current (and new) systems and 2) to acquire additional microprocessor systems.	30,000	30,000	30,000	3,000	3,000
C-CPS-5	To complete funding of previously approved CT-V position.	3,000	3,000	3,000	3,000	3,000
C-CPS-6	To acquire interactive computer system for student use.	95,000	10,000	10,000	10,000	10,000
C-CPS-7	To provide additional computer terminals for faculty use.	10,000	10,000	2,000	2,000	2,000

ESTIMATED ADDITIONAL FUNDS REQUIRED

Department/Unit __Computer Science__

C-CPS-8	To provide additional space and building modifications necessary for expanded 1) classroom computing laboratories and 2) adequate consulting areas for large enrollment introductory courses.	50,000	50,000	50,000	50,000	50,000
C-CPS-9	To appoint academic advisor.	12,000	12,000	12,000	12,000	12,000
C-CPS-10	To increase availability of self-paced instruction (1/2 FTE faculty plus two graduate assistants).	20,000	20,000	20,000	20,000	20,000
C-CPS-11	To expand lifelong education program (1/2 FTE).	10,000	10,000	10,000	10,000	10,000
C-CPS-12	To develop short courses through Continuing Education Service.	0	0	0	0	0
C-CPS-13	To develop graduate level project course to provide continuing CAI capabilities (1/4 FTE).	5,000	5,000	5,000	5,000	5,000

Comments:

1. The Change Plan is a structured display of objectives and additional funds required for the next five years. The objectives are listed in order of priority and revised each year.
2. On a preceding page, department chairmen are provided with an indication of how likely they are to get additional funds from the provost and dean.

Department/Unit Computer Science

Internal Resource Reallocation

Figure 10. 1977-78 Annual Evaluation and Report
Schedule A: Instructional Units

INTERNAL RESOURCE REALLOCATION

CHANGE OBJECTIVE AGAINST WHICH THE REALLOCATION IS APPLIED:	SOURCES OF REALLOCATIONS	POSSIBLE CONSEQUENCES
C-CPS-3	Shift some of Labor funds to Salary account. $9,200 by third year	With new funds, ability to acquire additional excellent graduate students.
C-CPS-12	Funded through course fees charged to participants.	Possible generation of additional funds for use in helping to meet department needs.

Comments:
In the change plan, each objective has a total cost which is broken down into an amount that the provost is asked to provide and an amount that can be provided by reallocation within the unit (the cost within the parentheses). This section of the AER is used to indicate how the unit plans to carry out these internal reallocations.

**Figure 11. 1977-78 Annual Evaluation and Report
Schedule A: Instructional Units**

Department/Unit __Philosophy__
Reduction Requested $ __8,300__

<u>Unit Flexibility Plan</u>

<u>UNIT FLEXIBILITY PLAN</u>

Department Code—Priority	OBJECTIVE Description	ANTICIPATED FLEXIBLE DOLLARS FY 78-79	FY 79-80
F-PHL-1	eliminate one .5 G.A.	$4,246	$4,246
F-PHL-2	eliminate one .5 G.A.	$4,246	$4,246

Comments:
Note that the format of the flexibility plan is identical to that of the change plan except that it plans for a budget reduction rather than a budget increase.

**Figure 12. 1977-78 Annual Evaluation and Report
Schedule A: Instructional Units**

List each of your Flexibility Plan objectives and follow it with a detailed discussion of the consequences which would ensue if the funds involved were withdrawn.

Department/Unit Philosophy

CONSEQUENCES OF FLEXIBILITY PLAN

Consequences of Flexibility Plan

Flexibility Plan Objectives (Department Code-Priority)	Consequence of Withdrawing Funds
F-PHL-1	Losing one half-time G.A. would not drastically affect our program, but would have an adverse effect on graduate student and faculty morale.
F-PHL-2	Losing two half-time G.A.'s would rather seriously affect our instructional program, especially if the loss continued beyond next year. Next fall, for example, we plan to hire 11 half-time G.A.'s for instructional purposes. Five will be used to staff sections for which we do not have faculty available, and the other six will assist in twelve other sections. If these six were reduced by two then four sections would be without assistants. The long range effects are even more distressing. Our 101 line is now $32,600, which will purchase about seven G.A.'s or a bit more than half of what we need. The rest we will hire from open money. If the 101 line is reduced by $8,300, to $24,300, then it would purchase only about five G.A.'s. During a year when we had little or no open money, it would be a complete disaster to our graduate program and our instructional program to try to operate with only 5 G.A.'s.

Comments:
This section ensures that the dean and the provost are aware of any adverse consequences connected with the withdrawal of the unit funds specified in the flexibility plan. Since many chairmen use this section to defend their budgets from reductions, rather than realistically presenting the repercussions, institutional researchers must indicate these consequences in light of the data and comment on any differences of opinion.

Figure 13. 1977-78 Annual Evaluation and Report Schedule A: Instructional Units

Department/Unit: Computer Science

FY 1978-79 Budget Request for Unit Change Plan

College or Administrative Unit: Engineering

Account Number: 11-272-

Department or Account Name: Computer Science

FY 1978-79 BUDGET REQUEST FOR UNIT CHANGE PLAN

Objective	FACULTY FTE	FACULTY $	A-P FTE	A-P $	C-T FTE	C-T $	CA FTE	CA $	LABOR $	SUP & SERV $	EQUIP $	TOTAL FTE	TOTAL $
C-CPS-1	2.0	40,000										2.0	40,000
C-CPS-2							1.0	14,400				1.0	14,400
C-CPS-3							2.5	22,000				2.5	22,000
C-CPS-4											30,000	--	30,000
C-CPS-5					0.3	3,000						0.3	3,000
C-CPS-6											95,000*	--	95,000
C-CPS-7											10,000	--	10,000
C-CPS-8										50,000**		--	50,000
C-CPS-9	1.0	12,000										1.0	12,000
C-CPS-10a	--	--											
C-CPS-11a	--	--											
C-CPS-12	--	--											
C-CPS-13a	--	--											
TOTAL	3.0	$52,000			0.3	$3,000	3.5	$36,400		$50,000	$135,000	6.8	$276,400

Comments:
Note that every budget line corresponds to a change plan objective requiring new funds.

Figure 14. 1977-78 Annual Evaluation and Report
Schedule C: Colleges and Major Administrative Units

College Arts and Letters

COLLEGE CHANGE PLAN

CONCEPTUAL OBJECTIVES		RELATED OPERATIONAL OBJECTIVES		ACCEPTABLE CONTRIBUTING UNIT GOALS	ESTIMATED ADDITIONAL FUNDS REQUIRED					
College Code–Priority	DESCRIPTION	College Code	Description		FY 1978-79	FY 1979-80	FY 1980-81	FY 1981-82	FY 1982-83	
C-A&L-1	To maintain & revitalize teaching and research competence in critical areas in strong degree programs.	C-A&L-1-I	To fill key vacant positions with younger faculty members	C-Mus	0 (13,500)	0 (13,500)	0 (13,500)	0 (13,500)	0 (13,500)	
				C-Eng	0 (14,000)	0 (14,000)	0 (14,000)	0 (14,000)	0 (14,000)	
				C-Eng-7	0	0	0 (15,000)	0 (15,000)	0 (15,000)	
				C-Hst-11	0	0	0 (15,000)	0 (15,000)	0 (15,000)	
				C-Phl-3	0	0	0 (15,000)	0 (15,000)	0 (15,000)	
				C-Rel-5	0	0	0 (15,000)	0 (15,000)	0 (15,000)	
				C-LOA-1	0 (7,500)	0 (7,500)	0 (7,500)	0 (7,500)	0 (7,500)	
				C-Mus	0 (14,000)	0 (14,000)	0 (14,000)	0 (14,000)	0 (14,000)	
			TOTALS		0 (49,000) 49,000	0 (49,000) 49,000	0 (109,000) 109,000	0 (109,000) 109,000	0 (109,000) 109,000	

Comments:

1. An example of a college change plan has been included to show how the broad conceptual objectives are broken into smaller operational objectives which in turn are described in terms of unit objectives that the dean feels would achieve his intended result. The conceptual objectives give the provost a sense of what the dean is attempting to do, whereas the breakdown to unit objectives allows him to see where any additional funds will flow.

2. A department chairman, in reading this college change plan and noting the placement of his unit within it, can easily perceive the dean's intentions and how the dean's priorities match or mismatch his own. Such a review of the college change plan by the unit directors and chairmen exerts a subtle influence that gradually brings department plans into closer alignment with the dean's priorities. To aid in this important process, every department chairman is given a copy of his dean's priorities. To aid in this important process, every department chairman is given a copy of his dean's change plan along with the AER materials. In some cases, the deans were sensitive about revealing their priorities to their chairmen and so it was necessary for the provost to take this decision off the hands of the deans.

planned objectives gained? Thus the new AER required that each unit administrator relate what progress had taken place with respect to each objective in his change plan (see Figure 8). The reports for those units receiving additional funds during the past year were more closely monitored than previously.

The more important details contained in each section of the AER can quickly be assimilated by reviewing the examples provided in the next section. Comments to aid the reader's interpretation and offer insights on selected tables are included at the bottom of each page.

Problems. The second phase of the AER development had successfully brought elements of planning into the process and linked them with evaluation and budgeting. This resulted in budget requests and allocations that followed a more purposeful pattern with a higher degree of consistency over the years.

In spite of these successes, one major problem remained unresolved. The structure of the process encouraged a continual pressure for growth. The budgetary trendline, in terms of consistent dollars, was always on an upward slope. As long as the process was initiated at the unit level with units asking for additional resources to support their own objectives, the momentum of the budget request was irresistible by the time it reached the provost. While the flexibility plans were used to reduce the budgets of some colleges, the dollars thus released were never enough to cover what was requested elsewhere. As predictions became more certain, an AER process unable to restrain growth seemed increasingly less acceptable. Premonitions of a financial crisis became strong enough by fiscal year 1978–1979 to begin the groundwork for yet another AER phase.

Phase 3 — A Budget Reduction Planning Process (1979-   )

The AER, as it now exists, was recently modified by a committee of representatives from the Provost's Office, Institutional Research, and the Budget Office. This group, meeting weekly over a period of six months, reformulated the AER process to focus the planning on reducing the academic budget while attempting to sustain program quality. One of the first tasks was to assess the future fiscal situation and express it in concrete, easily understandable terms. This was accomplished by means of a financial planning model, programmed and analyzed through the use of the modeling system recently developed by EDUCOM (Updegrove, 1978). Once the computer model was formulated and tested, the committee established certain reasonable assumptions regarding budget growth rates and used the model to obtain a series of five-year financial forecasts which were termed the optimistic, best-guess, and pessimistic cases. The forecasts for these three cases showed respectively larger deficits. These outcomes convincingly pictured a situation which up to this point manifested itself as a vague feeling of uneasiness. In a series of presentations, central administrators, deans, and faculty committees were apprised of the impending fiscal problem and prepared in advance for a new planning procedure primarily oriented toward reducing the academic staff and budget.

Concurrent with the modeling efforts, institutional researchers worked closely with the provost to design new AER schedules, formats, and procedures. The most important changes are as follows: (1) The data provided to units is considerably expanded. Units are given enrollment projections in courses, data showing section sizes in each course offered the previous term, and teaching loads for every faculty member. The focus of the data was changed by moving from an array of averages to a display of averages, ranges, and variances with the expectation that units must pay particular attention to data falling within the extremes of the range. (2) The emphasis was shifted from using the data for evaluation to using it to plan staffing. (3) Central administration provided the impetus toward a planned staff and budget reduction by means of staff and budget targets established for each college for each of the subsequent three years. (4) Deans are given increased planning autonomy. they develop the staff and budget targets required for all their units to meet the targets set for the colleges. (5) The establishment of dual targets — budget and staff — ensures that imbalances are not created by units seeking to preserve their staff by restricting their budget cutbacks to the supplies and services category. (6) The AER time schedule is accelerated so that colleges whose plans call for personnel reductions or additions have sufficient lead time to effect these changes by the next fiscal year. (7) If revenues exceed the planned expenditures for a given year, the provost will begin applying these funds to a series of university level projects that do not need the funds on a recurring basis.

This new AER procedure is still in the implementation phase but we feel that its successes will far outweigh any deficiencies. This judgment is predicated on its evolutionary development and the achievements of its predecessors. It is clear, however, that this goal-oriented style of planning could not even have been contemplated without the availability of data and a generation of administrators at all levels who have had ample experience in its use.

The increase in the complexity of the Phase 3 procedures necessitated wider participation at the department level and the addition of more frequent meetings between administrators at various levels. These changes are reflected in the flow diagram, Figure 15.

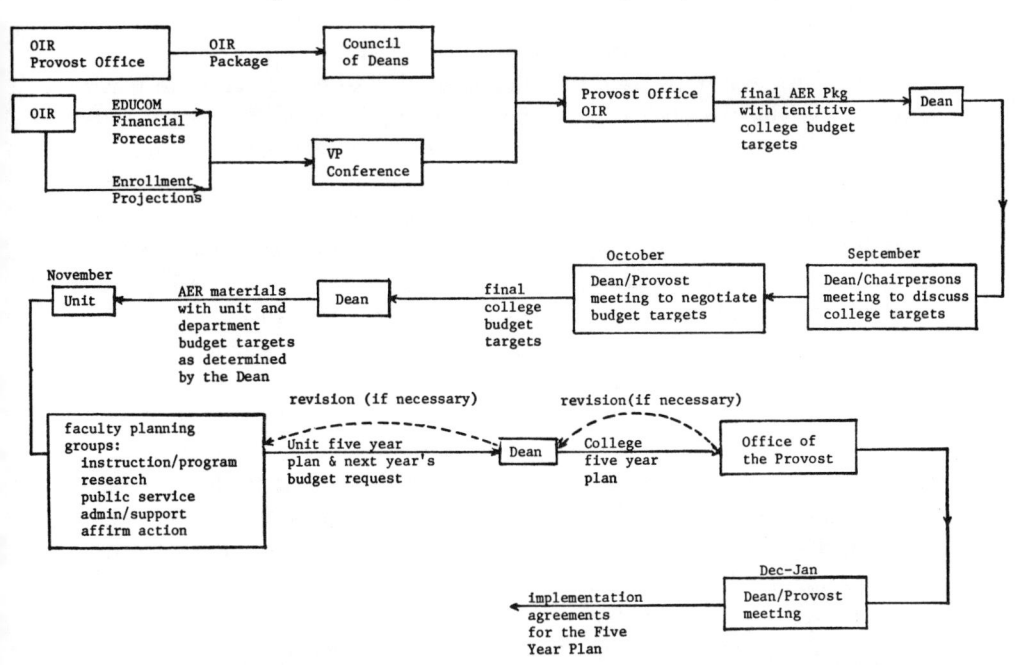

Figure 15. Annual Evaluation Cycle (Phase 3)

Lessons Learned

The preceding material traces one institution's experiences in grappling with the complex problem of how to effectively plan and budget. The narrative format was chosen as the best means of demonstrating that a planning system must be constantly modified in response to prevailing economic and political considerations. Since the focus of this chapter has been on the data to set standards, evaluate progress, assess plans, provide insights into complex operations, and maintain a close linkage between planning, budgeting, and reality, it may be helpful to make some observations on data usage and procedural matters before concluding with remarks of a broader nature.

Experiences with Data Usage. (1) Do not try to operate behind closed doors. Make all your evaluation methods public. (2) Allow space for units to express their reactions to the data and their concerns about the process in general. (3) Design the forms in order to separate comments about the accuracy of the data from comments about the interpretation of the data. (4) Let the deans play as large a role as possible in assessing their units and reacting to unit comments. (5) Strive for comprehensive evaluation. Do not focus only on instruction. (6) Do not become convinced that data are reality. Leave room for the introduction and consideration of subjective issues and maintain a certain amount of skepticism toward even the most reliable data. (7) Be alert to changes in the methods used to collect and process the data. Data processing systems are always undergoing change; a modification of the processing procedure can cause a change in a unit's data and be misinterpreted by an unwary analyst. (8) If a model is used in conjunction with the data, begin with a simple one whose operation can at least be outlined to inquiring chairpersons. (9) Try to standardize the format so people do not receive a completely alien report each year. (10) In an appendix define all terms and labels used on the data sheets and indicate the source documents. (11) Let people know which particular data elements figure heavily in the evaluation and hold workshops to demonstrate the interpretations that can be drawn from the figures. (12) When evaluating very dissimilar support units, it is better to develop special questions for each unit than to attempt to devise very general questions applicable to all units. (13) Bind the department data pages into well-tabbed binders and provide copies to all the key administrators. This will encourage them to use the data during the course of the year, which in turn cause the deans and chairpersons to adopt the same attitude toward the use of data. (14) It is important that the evaluation, planning, and budget processes be viewed as interrelated activities. This can be successful only if all three processes are handled within the same document. (15) Internal workload and productivity should be supplemented by external comparisons that the data collected from peer institutions. (16) Resist the impulse to give units an overall rating. It is more effective to give a separate evaluation rating to each major function since the purpose is in large part to promote change rather than to arrive at a final judgment of a program. Evaluators should not have to couch their final judgments in diplomatic or vague terms; the more concise and blunt the evaluators are, the more useful they become. (17) Attempt to have funds allocated at the same level on which the evaluations are made — where departments are evaluated, much effort is undone if the funds are distributed to the colleges without suggestions as to how these funds should be allocated to the departments. (18) If the number of data pages is so great as to limit their use, develop a summary sheet for each unit. Try to involve the use of these summary sheets in as many ongoing functions as possible. (19) No matter what efforts are made to control the growth of the data section, the pages will multiply each year. At the very minimum, prune out every data block that went unused in the previous year's report. (20) Use the computer to its fullest potential. The more time staff must spend on handling data, the less time they will have for analyzing it. (21) Establish a timetable for the planning and budgeting process and make every effort to adhere to it. After a point, additional time does not result in any improvements to the end product. (22) The data does not necessarily speak for itself. A good format is important—a densely packed page of figures loses much of its effectiveness since nothing can possibly catch the eye and few people will even attempt to examine it closely. (23) One of the major, initial problems that must be surmounted is a strong impression at the unit level that no one at higher levels really reads and follows up on these reports. Any feedback to the units on suggestions they make or questions they raise will help dispel this feeling. (24) The deans are apt to be the major group needing assistance in appreciating how such a procedure can improve operations. If they are functioning only as conveyor belts between the units and central administration, the procedures and planning formats must be redesigned so as to force the deans to become more actively involved in the evaluation, planning, and budgeting process. (25) There is a tendency for chairpersons and deans to focus on the data rather than the underlying problems. Central administrators must disengage from arguments about the data and center the discussions on whether certain problems exist and, if they do exist, what is being done about them.

Reflections on Institutional Level Planning. In the foregoing discussion, the attention paid to data-related matters may seem to be out of proportion to what is customarily regarded as the larger problem of how to plan. This has been deliberate. The essential elements of planning, as we see it, are data, procedures, and the participants—all very mundane in comparison to the lavish documents that are frequently displayed as evidence of good planning and which contain global pronouncements of goals and missions. University goal and mission statements are nothing more than broad aspirations—many times too vague or all-encompassing to serve any useful purpose except to officially sanction every activity carried on in the name of the university and thus placate the various interest groups both internal and external to the university.

In our opinion planning requires two major ingredients: a short list of precisely defined university goals, and a means of transforming these goals into action. Of these, we have found the latter to be the harder, the more unpleasant, and, presumably for these reasons, the more neglected in the many university planning systems which have been reviewed. For this reason the narration is focused on the abstruse problem of how one transforms an abstract goal into the hundreds of daily, unit level decisions that can eventually lead to its achievement. This imbalance in the foregoing narration is not meant to imply that establishing university level goals is either unimportant or easy. In fact, during the initial stages of the third phase of the AER, six months were consumed in such efforts.

The following comments reflect our experiences with developing university level goals over a six-year period: (1) Clearly stated university goals of a type that can be put into operation will only result if the problems facing the university are presented with equal precision. We have found that enrollment and financial computer models are a wondrously effective means through which to focus attention on the concrete details of potential problems. (2) It is best to keep planning goals internal to the university. As soon as they become public statements about where the institution is headed, they begin to accumulate the superfluous baggage associated with public relations pronouncements. (3) Open communications with the academic community are imperative. It is impossible to repeat too often the university planning goals or to overexplain the necessity for them. (4) If the problem facing the university is a financial one, and increasingly it seems to be, the options should be expressed in terms of tradeoffs. For example, if tuition is to be held fixed then faculty salaries cannot increase at an inflationary rate; if certain colleges must be given additional support then others must suffer a reduction in support. Until administrators at all levels begin to think of the university as a closed system, which necessitates tradeoffs, they are mentally burdened with the erroneous impression that there are optimal solutions with no unpleasant side effects. In its more serious form, this misconception leads to paralysis. Computer models are excellent tools for demonstrating the effects of various constraints and the give-and-take nature of most solutions. (5) The portion of the academic budget amenable to spontaneous reallocation within any given year is shockingly small, perhaps 2 or 3 percent. This implies that goals can only be approached in small steps over long time intervals. Such a situation demands careful long-range planning (four to six years) that effects certain progress year after year and is not impeded or realigned according to current, temporary problems. (6) In times of constrained budgets, the concept of change cannot be considered synonymous with growth. New programs and improvements to existing programs can no longer be funded as budget additions. They must be accomodated by a corresponding decrease somewhere else in the budget. In this way, the perpetual thrust toward innovation and change can be used constructively to overcome the pressure for maintaining the status quo within outdated or ineffective programs and units.

The future suggests that planning will require a serious and constrained attempt at defining more clearly the goal and mission of the institution and its units. This will entail an equally honest attempt to get administrators and faculty to deal with planning, not as an exercise divorced from daily life, nor as an academic parlor game played by arguing the structure of a sentence in the mission statement or by dissecting the data, but rather as a serious procedure for planning the use of limited resources. Good planning is reflected in the effective use of human resources—not by brochures, data, or good intentions. Certainly future planning will require the talents of statisticians, institutional researchers, and budget analysts; however, if we are to be successful as educational managers we must also have skilled and knowledgeable people who can, under severe restraints, plan for program development and utilize organizational and human relations skills to motivate and organize scarce human resources into a forward-looking effort during a period of public neglect and indifference. Rather than further refining data elements, formats, analysis, and mission statements, we need to refine in a more effective manner the way we conduct the business of instruction, research, and public service. Unless this challenge is taken up we will have developed more and better theories of planning, but we will not have increased the quality of programs and may have unwittingly aided in the decline of higher education.

References

Dressel, P., and Simon, L. A. K. (Ed.). *New Directions for Institutional Research: Allocating Resources Among Departments,* no. 11. San Francisco: Jossey-Bass, 1976.

Updegrove, D. A. "EFPM—The EDUCOM Financial Model." *EDUCOM Bulletin.* Princeton, N.J.: EDUCOM, Winter 1978.

Thomas M. Freeman is associate vice-chancellor at the State University of New York and is former director of, and professor in, the Office of Institutional Research at Michigan State University. He is particularly interested in planning and budgeting systems for governmental agencies, having served as a member of the Michigan Higher Education Funding Model Task Force and as a consultant to SUNY and the Department of the Army.

William A. Simpson is associate professor in the Office of Institutional Research and adjunct associate professor of mathematics in Lyman Briggs Residential College at Michigan State University. He has a special interest in the application of administrative science techniques to higher education.

When real resources decline, demands change, or programs lose vitality, then a logical move is to reallocate resources to facilitate academic planning.

Resource Allocation: Stopgap or Support for Academic Planning?

R. Sue Mims

Management of decline is a role in which many of us are engaged today and one we must face in the foreseeable future. The challenge is, in part, one of preventing decline in the quality of academic programs while coping with a decline in resources. In the past most of our planning, budgeting, and management strategies have been predicated on assumptions of continuing growth of faculty, students, and dollars. Further, most of us are conditioned to evaluate organizational performance and individual satisfaction in growth terms. As Levine (1978) has noted, when faced with the prospects of decline, we typically begin with measures designed to stem the decline, and only as the trend persists are we moved to employ more adaptive means for coping with it. A study of the "new depression in higher education" indicated that institutions typically respond to financial difficulty in five general ways: postponing expenditures, belt-tightening, marginal reallocation of resources, increasing income, and planning and worrying (Cheit, 1971).

The author is indebted to Thomas A. Karman for his insights on the Oklahoma State University Excellence Fund.

The management of decline occupies much current thinking and writing (Cyert, 1975; Mortimer and Tierney, 1979). However, it would be unproductive to let this theme dominate a more balanced perspective, because some institutions have current and continuing opportunities for growth, and many more have healthy prospects for the following decades. Given these conditions, what planning and management approaches are likely to be effective? One institutional management response, resource reallocation, is singled out for discussion in this chapter.

Reallocation schemes and experiences at the University of Michigan–Ann Arbor and Oklahoma State University are described and compared. Because different circumstances led to the introduction of resource reallocation at these campuses, these examples permit contrasts of reallocation as a response to decline and as a response to opportunity. The relationship between reallocation and planning is also explored.

In this context resource reallocation is defined as the movement of money, personnel (or positions), space, or equipment from one unit to another. Planning is broadly conceived as those processes by which an institution develops approaches and procedures for choosing its future, and for making progress toward reaching it.

The University of Michigan Priority Fund

After a period of sustained growth in students, faculty, and budgets in the 1960s, the University of Michigan began to face the prospect of decline in the 1970s. Total enrollment on the Ann Arbor campus peaked in mid decade. The rate of increase in state support slowed as the state suffered economic difficulties. Institutional cost increases reduced management flexibility. In response to these conditions the University of Michigan made a series of ad hoc across-the-board budget reductions and reallocations. Tuition and fees were increased significantly. Expenditures for maintenance and equipment were trimmed or deferred.

By 1977 it was clear that many expenditures could no longer be delayed. Nearly all slack in the budget had been depleted. Little money for new programs was available from the state or other external sources. Sober appraisal led university officials to look for other strategies for maintaining or improving the quality of programs over the coming decade within a stable real-dollar budget. A differential, multiyear reallocation procedure called the Priority Fund was implemented.

The introduction of the Priority Fund was not the only response in the university. This reallocation fund was part of a larger evaluation and planning effort that had been initiated several years before. Schools and colleges developed statements of objectives, set enrollment targets, negotiated broad planning agreements with the Office of Academic Affairs, and established evaluation plans. The Priority Fund was introduced as one means of assisting units in implementing plans.

Purposes and Rationale. The purposes and rationale of the Priority Fund were set forth for the academic community in late 1977. "University programs and priorities will continue to evolve in accord with the interests of students and faculty, the development of new areas of knowledge, and the interests of society. It is vital that the university maintain its ability, even through periods of stable real-dollar budgets, to adapt to these changing interests, as well as to assist existing programs which are, in view of our priorities, relatively underfunded. Budgetary flexibility is an essential ingredient of the ability to respond to both of these challenges" (*Priority Fund,* 1977, p. 1). Thus, the Priority Fund was established both to respond to changing interests and opportunities, and to provide greater support for existing programs of high priority.

Design and Phase-In. The Priority Fund was designed as a three-year experiment, subject to continuation after evaluation. In effect an annual tax was placed on base budgets. By reducing each unit's base General Fund budget by an amount equal to 1 percent of the previous year's budget, a pool of approximately $1.5 million would be generated annually. These dollars would then be available for reallocation into the *base budgets* of selected units.

Certain budget categories were excluded from the annual Priority Fund reductions: staff benefits, purchased utilities, and mandatory transfers. Further, since budgets were tight due to prior reductions and effects of inflation, the decision was made to phase in the "tax." Thus, in the first year (1978-79) the General Fund instruction and research budgets of academic units would be reduced by only one third of 1 percent of their previous year's budget; all other budgets would be subject to the full 1 percent reduction with the exceptions noted above. In the second year (1979-80) schools and colleges would contribute two thirds of 1 percent of their 1978-79 base; all other units would provide 1 percent. Finally, in the third year (1980-81) all units would be subject to the full 1 percent reduction of their 1979-80 base. Thus, in the three successive years a reallocation pool of approximately $1 million, $1.3 million, and $1.5 million would be generated.

The phase-in feature of the reallocation program was also instituted to allow schools and colleges adequate time to plan, recognizing that many had relatively low instructional staff turnover and required a long lead time to appoint new faculty.

It is important to note that at the University of Michigan budget allocations are made to vice-presidential areas and major units such as schools and colleges. In turn, schools and colleges decide on allocations to departments. For the Priority Fund, each vice-president and dean would determine whether the reductions would be across-the-board or whether differential shares would be determined through more sophisticated means.

The Priority Fund Reallocation Process. The reallocation process is initiated with units making specific requests to the vice-president for Academic Affairs. These requests are discussed in the annual planning/budgeting conference between each dean, director, and vice-president and the vice-president for Academic Affairs. The vice-president for Academic Affairs then formulates and discusses draft recommendations with the Budget Priorities Committee, a representative group of faculty, administrators, and students. Recommendations for distribution are then made by the vice-president for Academic Affairs to the Committee on Budget Administration (the executive officers) which makes the final reallocation decisions. Notification of Priority Fund distributions are made no later than June for the new fiscal year beginning July 1. Distribution decisions are made public.

Units also have the opportunity to request and receive allocations from the fund spanning more than one fiscal year. For example, in Fall 1978 a unit might request dollars for equipment for fiscal year 1980 and for fiscal year 1981. In turn the unit might receive notification in Spring 1979 of an allocation for fiscal year 1980 from the current pool and for fiscal year 1981 from the following year's pool. Such out-year allocations enable units to engage in fiscal planning and personnel recruitment with greater certainty.

From the beginning central policy has excluded the possibility of meeting certain budgetary needs through the Priority Fund: (1) university-wide faculty and staff compensation programs, (2) university-wide nonsalary inflation offsetting programs, and (3) utility increases. Beyond these exclusions units have been given few request guidelines. Schools and colleges have been expected to make requests in accord with prior planning agreements reached with the vice-president for Academic Affairs. Also, units have been required to inform the vice-president where the Priority Fund reductions will be taken and are not permitted to immediately request reallocations for the same purposes. That is, a unit cannot make its contributions from an equipment account, indicating it has low priority, and then request reallocation funds for equipment as a high priority.

In the first year criteria to be used in making reallocation decisions from the Priority Fund were announced. These criteria are shown

in Table 1. Prior to the second year of the Priority Fund the vice-president for Academic Affairs identified critical university level needs that units were asked to take into consideration in making their requests and plans. These high priority needs included:
- A better internal balance among items and activities financed by the General Fund
- Competititve faculty salaries
- A well-qualified student body of adequate size
- Increased flexibility in General Fund budgets
- Increased allocations to equipment, plant renovation, and library acquisitions
- Further development of external sources of support, including sponsored research and public and private gifts and grants

The overall goal set forth by the Office of Academic Affairs is to maintain and improve the intellectual quality of its education, research, and service programs. These critical times, while disturbing, are viewed as presenting opportunities for creative evaluation and redirection of the activities in which the university is engaged. The challenge is one of

Table 1. Priority Fund Allocation Criteria
The University of Michigan

1. Centrality of the program to the university, viewed in terms of its pertinence to and support of the growth, preservation, and communication of knowledge.
2. Current and projected future societal demands for graduates and/or services of the program.
3. The effect of the program upon the university's relationship with the government, with the community, and with other universities, as well as its contribution toward the university's legally required compliance with state and federal statutes.
4. The current reputation and quality of the program, considering national ratings, professional accreditation standards, research productivity, qualification of entering students, quality of graduate placement, attrition of students.
5. The program's impact upon other areas of the university, its contribution toward the support of primary programs of instruction and/or research, and the extent of services required by the program from other areas of the university.
6. Anticipated level of enrollment in the program.
7. The program's contribution toward the fiscal viability of the university, the degree to which the program is self-sufficient, the present level of outside funding which it attracts, and future projections regarding the availability of such funding.
8. Levels of faculty and staff workloads within the program, resulting from uncontrollable external circumstances, or from internal program development.
9. The program's contribution to the mental and physical well-being of the university community.

focusing resources effectively and remaining flexible and innovative despite constraints on finances (*Resource Planning and Academic Excellence,* 1978; Shapiro, 1978). The Priority Fund reallocation is one approach to assist in achieving these goals and objectives.

Problems, Strengths, and Results. How have units behaved in identifying contributions and requesting allocations? Have significant reallocations occurred? Has the Priority Fund facilitated academic program planning at the unit level? Has it supported institutional planning?

In designing the Priority Fund some people suggested forming the pool by taking the money "off the top" of the state appropriation and tuition revenue. The weakness of this approach is in its not directly and immediately forcing units to reconsider priorities, to identify new opportunities, and to reallocate their resources. In other words, an "off the top" approach is less likely to change behavior.

The processes by which deans and directors have made reductions have varied greatly. Some heads have passed along across-the-board cuts to programs and departments. Others have made differential cuts, with nonsalary accounts generally reduced first even though that area has been generally underfunded relative to salaries. During the first year, large schools and colleges tended to absorb much of the Priority Fund reduction in central collegiate accounts. However, in the second year colleges began to extract a greater and differential portion from subsidiary units. Knowing two to three years in advance that they were going to be subject to reductions, collegiate and departmental units have been faced with the prospect of planning for leaner programs. In larger schools and colleges in particular, decisions about reductions, requests, and allocations have required lengthy consultation through the established governance processes.

Unit requests for Priority Fund allocations have not been strikingly different from normal budget requests (nor should they necessarily be). There have been more requests for faculty and staff than for nonsalary items, and more requests for enhancing existing programs than for new programs. Further, the bulk of the requests have been for a single year (recognizing, however, that an allocation would be continued in successive bases) rather than for multiple years. More instructional units have submitted requests for Priority Fund support than have noninstructional areas.

In the first year units made separate requests for Priority Funds and for programs to be submitted to the state. However, in retrospect, they were not given sufficient guidelines to determine what might best qualify for the Priority Fund and what ought to be sent to the state. In following years, units have submitted all requests to the vice-president for Academic Affairs without specifying a funding source. Determination of the most appropriate funding source has then been made by the Committee on Budget Administration.

Clearly one issue in reallocation schemes is by whom and how decisions are to be made. Should decisions be made by line administrators (if so, at what levels) or by a standing or ad hoc committee? Should students be involved? What should be the role of statements of priorities and criteria, and the role of informed judgment relative to quantitative analysis? The University of Michigan came out clearly for line decision making, using the benefit of advice from a standing committee (headed by faculty).

Initial recommendations for Priority Fund allocations are made by the vice-president for Academic Affairs, and are sent to the Budget Priorities Committee (with faculty, student, and administrative representation) for review and advice. Although central level decision criteria (Table 1) have been articulated, administrators and faculty alike have found that criteria are difficult if not impossible to apply in any explicit way to specific requests. Nor have the decisions been supported by extensive analysis of the requests. Historical trend information and comparative peer information have provided the background for the reallocation decisions more often than have separate, in-depth analyses. In brief, then, decisions have been largely judgmental, guided in general rather than in particular by criteria and quantitative analysis.

Reallocation has been accomplished. In the first two years, as the Fund has been phased in, noninstitutional budgets have been taxed more heavily than instructional budgets. Also, schools and colleges have received much more from the Fund than have support units. A need recognized by the central administration, and by some units, was to move dollars from salary to nonsalary uses. To accomplish this objective and to provide incentives, the central administration has given multiyear grants to selected units for equipment. The understanding is that units will match the Priority Fund allocations with further internal reallocation, thereby building up the equipment accounts more rapidly.

Academic program planning has been facilitated both from the central perspective and from the collegiate point of view. Knowing that reductions would have to be made at least for three successive years, units have been forced to engage in more long-term academic and fiscal planning and to retain some budget flexibility. The Fund has given the schools and colleges more leverage with programs and departments; here reallocation has been played out largely in terms of reallocation of faculty positions. Priority Fund allocations have contributed to the implementation of program plans for some units by providing a vital margin of new dollars. Of course, academic units not receiving allocations have not been able to implement many desired changes. On the other hand, some nonacademic units, operating in part on recharges, increased their fees in order to make up for Priority Fund reductions. Clearly this behavior, until monitored and controlled, subverted the purposes of the Priority Fund.

A continuing problem has been the timing of Priority Fund allocations. When the Fund was introduced requests were made in early winter for the coming fiscal year, and allocations were made only one or two months before the beginning of the fiscal year. By that point it was usually difficult if not impossible for units to engage in successful faculty recruiting and programming for the new year. The response to this problem has been to move the initial request and planning/budgeting conferences back from the winter to early fall, before the primary faculty search season. Then efforts have been made to distribute a portion of the Priority Fund in the fall so that units may begin recruiting with assurance of funding. However, with the prospect of midyear funding cutbacks from the state, it has not always been possible to make early distributions.

The Future of the Priority Fund. In an assessment of recent evaluation and planning efforts, deans and directors have given favorable ratings to the Priority Fund. A more systematic evaluation and a decision about the future of the Fund will be made in 1980.

The overall goal of the Fund is to maintain and enhance program quality; specific objectives are to respond to new opportunities and to support more generously existing programs of high priority. To some extent these objectives have been accomplished. However, problems and questions remain. To date emphasis has been placed on looking at the contribution of reallocations to objectives. Little attention has been given to analyzing the ability of various units to make Priority Fund contributions, nor has the impact of these reductions on program quality been studied. In order to remain effective over the long run, the impact of reductions as well as allocations must be factored into the equation.

The Oklahoma State University Excellence Fund

As an institution in a "sun belt" state, Oklahoma State University (OSU) maintained strong enrollments in the 1970s, and suffered no unusual financial crises. However, the state of Oklahoma has not been generous in its support for higher education. Thus, it became apparent that if the university wanted to depart significantly from former paths, dollars would have to be generated from other sources—probably from internal sources.

In the early 1970s Oklahoma State was scheduled to undergo a decennial accreditation review. The university decided to capitalize on the accreditation period by engaging in a nontraditional self-study, one that "attempted seriously and systematically to analze the present in order to forge plans for the future" (Robl, Karman, and Boggs, 1976). It was clear that it would be necessary to reallocate resources in order to implement new plans. Thus, a pool of money called the Excellence Fund was garnered through budget reductions, and procedures for reallocating resources were developed.

The reallocation fund was linked to the three evaluation and planning stages of the self-study. The three phases included (1) program description, (2) analysis, development, and priority setting, and (3) consideration of alternative funding levels. Central questions addressed included: What are you currently doing? Should you be doing other things? What are your priorities? What would you do with less, more, or stable resources? (A more complete description of the self-study and planning efforts has been set forth by Robl, Karman, and Boggs, 1976.)

Purposes and Rationale. The university's goal was to increase the quality and vitality of its programs, and to develop a continuing planning process. The university intended each of its major units to develop plans that would enable them to achieve special excellence in selected areas. Further, it was expected that all services and activities carried out should be of acceptable quality if they were to be continued.

Quality for OSU has had two dimensions: the desirability of programs from a faculty member's perspective and from a larger university and societal perspective, and the effectiveness of the programs and their delivery. Vitality has also been conceived along two dimensions: the way the university responds to its environment and circumstances—exhibiting receptivity, flexibility, and resilience—and the internal climate which facilitates the effective development and delivery of programs and services (Robl, Karman, and Boggs, 1976).

Rather than depending completely on acquiring new dollars from external sources, a multiyear program of internal reallocations was established. The basic concept was to integrate planning and budgeting by implementing plans with dollars reallocated from the Excellence Fund. This fund was viewed as a "bootstrap operation designed to concentrate enough seed money as developmental capital to allow a part of the university to progress rapidly, to gain national visibility, and to be able to 'go it alone' " (Robl, Karman, and Boggs, 1976, p. 5).

Design and Phase-In. The Excellence Fund was phased in over a three-year period, with the exception that it would be revolving and ongoing. The intention of the plan was to acquire a pool of dollars by taxing Educational and General (E and G) budgets of major areas and units (such as president, vice-presidents, schools and colleges, and support units) by an amount equivalent to 2 percent, 4 percent, and then 6 percent of a baseline year. That is, if a college had a $2 million budget in FY 1975 (the base year), in FY 1977 it would be assessed 2 percent of the FY 1975 budget ($40,000); in FY 1978 an amount equivalent to 4 percent of the FY 1975 budget would be extracted ($80,000); and finally, 6 percent of the unit's FY 1975 budget ($120,000) would be recouped in FY 1979. Although the budget of each major unit was assessed at a flat rate each year, the administrator (for example, dean) responsible for that budget could amass the assessment by tapping subunit (for example, department) budgets at differential rates. Consequently, a high priority department could experience budgetary growth at the same time that lower priority departments were losing funds through heavier assessments.

The Excellence Fund was designed to support two separate grant programs. Some reallocation decisions would be made centrally; the Presidential Challenge Grant fund was designated to support special programs that would bring national attention and recognition to the university in selected areas. This part of the fund then was to facilitate achieving special areas of eminence for the university as a whole. Other parts of the fund would go to Vice-President's and Dean's Incentive Grant programs. These monies, reallocated by the individual deans and vice-presidents, were designed to support high-prioity programs within the respective administrative areas. The hope was that these reallocations would likewise enhance the quality and vitality of programs, bringing further distinction to the university. With the Excellence Fund fully operational, half of the resources would flow to the president for university-wide reallocation and half would be retained within the major units (vice-presidents, deans) for internal reallocation.

The Excellence Fund Reallocation Process. The Excellence Fund concept was designed and most strongly supported by the vice-president for Academic Affairs and Research and the president. Support from other key administrators was garnered by giving them a significant role and providing them a pool of money for reallocation. The planning process began at the grassroots level with the specification of departmental priorities, then collegiate priorities, and, eventually, university priorities.

The planning and reallocation model has six steps: Each unit describes existing programs; unit priorities are established, including proposed new programs; priority lists flow up the administrative organization, with each present unit reordering programs in view of its own priorities; each unit outlines what programs it would carry out with more, less, or stable units, and these statements flow up the administrative organization; through the Excellence Fund tax, money is collected and redistributed, then allocations are made within the framework of three-year plans; after a specified time period, funds are gradually removed and reallocated to other programs or projects (Robl, Karman, and Boggs, 1976, p. 5). After completing an initial cycle of all six steps — description, analysis, priority setting, consideration of alternatives, collection of funds, and reallocation — the process has in subsequent years focused on the last two steps.

Initially, six basic university level areas of excellence were chosen for emphasis over the decade. Departmental and collegiate plans that aligned with university level priorities or areas of emphasis were to be supported with reallocated dollars from the Excellence Fund. The multiyear awards were viewed as developmental. Rather than becoming part of the continuing base budget, reallocations constituted seed money, which was guaranteed for two or three years and then phased out as external funding was located to support the effort or as the unit adjusted budgets to maintain the effort; in some cases projects were terminated because evaluations found they did not warrant further institutional support.

Since the initiation of the Excellence Fund in 1976, the university has garnered some new dollars through enrollment growth and state appropriations. Units have been encouraged to channel these dollars into high priority areas along with dollars from the Excellence Fund. Also, since the fund's implementation there has been a change in the presidency and in other administrative leadership. As a result, some priorities have changed.

Criteria and Priorities. Criteria and priorities were central to the implementation of the Excellence Fund. At the beginning of the process units were provided with six criteria to be used in evaluating programs and establishing unit priorities: (1) centrality to the university mission, (2) productivity, (3) demand, (4) resources used, (5) vitality, and (6) uniqueness (Robl, Karman, and Boggs, 1976, p. 3).

Priorities were established beginning at the grass roots level and were integrated at each successive level as shown earlier. The overall objectives were to achieve areas of special excellence for the university as a whole and for each unit, and to continue to provide services at acceptable quality levels.

Problems, Strengths, and Results. The university capitalized on the scheduled reaccreditation by piggybacking on a planning and reallocation process. To garner vital support for the approach, key administrators were given responsibility for reallocating portions of the Excellence Fund. Further, in the beginning strong efforts were made to sketch the complete process and to inform participants at every step along the way. A spirit of openness and adaptability prevailed. As the need arose to make changes in the process, extensive discussions took place, and once decisions were made all participants were informed.

At Oklahoma State units resisted, or at least had difficulty in, setting priorities. Rather than forcing an explicit ranking, administrators accepted programs groups into "high," "medium," and "low" priority categories. Units were subject to successive 2 percent, 4 percent, and 6 percent budget reductions. In the early years many units tried to get by merely on a slimmer base. However, in the face of 12 percent reductions or more, units eventually were forced to engage in bonafide priority setting and internal reallocation.

In the beginning priorities and themes supported from the Excellence Fund were those that emerged from the grass roots level. As priorities have evolved, administrators have not automatically allocated money to the highest priority programs. Rather, the principle of marginal funding has been applied, putting dollars where administrators judged they would have the most impact, whether or not these were the highest priority items.

A strength and weakness of the reallocation and planning effort was comprehensiveness. Because of wide participation the process was very time consuming and at the beginning moved very slowly. In succeeding years the process has been streamlined. A side benefit of the process has been increased communication and coordination among units, and between units and the central administration.

At its outset some doubted that the effort would result in reallocation. Eventually it became clear to all that significant reallocation had occurred. Morale issues had to be dealt with at each step. The task of deciding what to cut was a difficult one, and was followed by the unpleasant experience of accepting the implications of the cuts. Morale declined in those units not receiving reallocations in the early years, although in recent years morale has improved as the last reductions have been made and as more units have received allocations. Some units funded by recharges have attempted to increase prices to offset Excellence Fund cuts.

The critical test as Oklahoma State was whether the process facilitated ongoing academic program planning. In the estimation of university officials (Robl, Karman, and Boggs, 1976) the process has overcome a common failure in planning by successfully linking planning and budgeting through the reallocation scheme. Further, they conclude that by integrating university level themes, special projects, and three-year plans, they have institutionalized a process that will facilitate the identification of and adaptation to emerging needs.

Summary and Conclusions

The Priority Fund and the Excellence Fund. The decisions to reallocate resources emerged from different circumstances at the two institutions under consideration in this chapter. After a period of sustained growth in the 1960s, Michigan began to face the prospect of decline in the 1970s. The Priority Fund was introduced, along with planning activities, to achieve budget flexibility. This flexibility was viewed as central, enabling the university to maintain its high-quality priority programs and to respond to changing interests and opportunities. In contrast, Oklahoma State had prospects for advancement and a strong determination to gain national visibility and to achieve excellence in special areas. To accomplish its objectives, Oklahoma State University developed the Excellence Fund to support its new directions.

Both reallocation schemes have been designed as multiyear, ongoing ventures. The Michigan Priority Fund has been financed through a small continuing tax on annual budgets; reallocations have been channeled back into the base budgets of units. The Oklahoma State Excellence Fund has been supported by a three-year tax on budgets of a baseline year; once amassed, the fund has been used as seed money or venture capital rather than being reallocated into base budgets. Thus, an ongoing tax is not extracted, but a continuous pool of resources has been established. As support for projects is phased out, resources become available to support new efforts.

The Priority Fund and Excellence Fund have both been conceptually and operationally linked with other systematic academic planning efforts. Bona fide reallocation has resulted in both instances. Shifts have occurred at the institutional program level (for example, flow of funds to instructional from noninstructional areas), at the collegiate and department level (such as, reallocation of faculty positions from one department or program to another), and among expenditure categories (from salaries and wages to equipment and supplies).

In both instances the reduction and reallocation processes have been generally open and participatory, though ultimate decisions have been made administratively and not by ad hoc or standing committees. At Michigan, the results are viewed in academic circles as being fair, but the reallocation process remains somewhat a mystery to those outside of the central administration. Both institutions met resistance to efforts at placing programs or activities in strict priority order and had difficulty in applying decision criteria to specific cases. Decisions have been made as much, if not more, on the basis of informed judgment than on systematic quantitative analysis.

As with almost any budgetary approach, these reallocation efforts have been subject to some gamesmanship. For example, some units initially offered up programs central to other units in the hope that they would not be cut. Other units operating on fees or recharges have tried to raise their charges to offset reductions. On the balance, academic areas have probably fared as well or better than nonacademic areas in the two cases, though this is by no means inherent in such reallocation schemes.

Stopgap or Support for Planning? At the core the need to reallocate resources is an indication that existing budget and planning systems are inadequate or ineffective. Resources are most often allocated in an incremental manner; alternatively, institutions engage in selective, ad hoc reallocation. Some institutions operating in a nonincremental fashion adopt more of a natural selection or marketplace strategy, while yet another approach to resource allocation is one more closely linked to planning, a priority-based system which results in differential allocation or reallocation on an ongoing basis. Reallocation efforts may serve either as a stopgap measure or as a bona fide support for academic planning.

The need to achieve long-term financial equilibrium has been noted (Mortimer and Tierney, 1979). That is, the budget must be balanced, but, also, the rate of increase in expenditures must be matched by the rate of increase in revenues. Ad hoc reallocations are often aimed at balancing the budget in a given year, and do not address long-term equilibrium. Thus, reallocation is often a stopgap measure, and balancing the budget an ultimate goal. The reallocation procedures implemented at Oklahoma State University and the University of Michigan do have links to academic planning. These resource reallocation schemes are not *planning*, rather they are *planning tools*. In neither case described did the introduction of the reallocation fund represent an attempt to bring about fundamental reform in flawed budget systems. To a degree, then, the reallocation procedures addressed symptoms rather than problems. The reallocation efforts have clearly supported academic planning over several years. It remains to be seen whether or not reallocations will help reduce rates of increase in expenditures and assist in achieving longer term financial equilibrium.

All Things Considered. Reallocation plans are most often implemented in times of financial stress, but are equally appropriate in growth conditions. Given renewed consideration of reallocation, it is worthwhile to summarize some of what has been learned at Oklahoma State, Michigan, and other institutions. These factors seem to be important: objectives; environmental and organizational conditions; the "tax;" time span and timing; people; linkage of the reallocation process to existing planning and budget systems; analysis and supporting information; and control and evaluation processes.

1. The reallocation approaches of Michigan and Oklahoma State depended at the outset on organizational flexibility. Institutional policies permitted the planned transfer of dollars from one expenditure category to another (for example, from salary to nonsalary). State policies likewise permitted the transfer of funds among organizational units and expenditure categories, and did not require the return of unexpended funds.

2. To be effective the objectives of reallocation must be clear and there must be some agreement on the desired ends. Is it the objective to balance the budget, to support new programs, or to better support existing programs? Attention needs to be given to linking the reallocation process, a tool, with ongoing budget and planning (academic and financial) systems; they should be serving congruent objectives, if not the same objectives.

3. In order to initiate reallocation, there must be knowledge of and agreement on financial circumstances, agreement that "we have a problem," or an "opportunity." Further, there must be agreement that *differential* action is required and support for the proposed readjustment *process*. Wide participation in designing and running the process often enhances support, as does operating in an open and unhurried manner. Serious efforts to set forth priorities and decision criteria and to link analysis and judgment are desirable, though difficult to achieve.

4. An important consideration in any reallocation scheme is the "tax" percentage or the amount of the fund to be amassed. The appropriate figures will vary from institution to institution, depending on budgetary slack and economic conditions. The amount reduced should be sufficiently large to cause bonafide change in activities, and not so small that the same activities can merely be pursued on a smaller base. Further, the amount reallocated must be sufficiently large to make a measurable difference in results.

5. The time span is one key to successful reallocation. If objectives are to link reallocation, academic planning, and financial planning, then a one-year, one-shot effort is inadequate to the task. Likewise, the timing of reallocation in relation to economic conditions is also important. It is difficult to initiate and maintain an ongoing reallocation process in the face of rapidly changing financial conditions. If resources increase significantly, then it becomes easier to avoid true reallocation. On the other hand, it there is a sudden, severe decline in real resources (for example, due to an unexpected increase in inflation), the original reallocation plan may be inadequate to or inappropriate for the new conditions.

6. People are central to successful implementation. Leadership and skilled management is required at all levels. Reduction and reallocation are more than the mere movement of resources. They impact and are impacted by attitudes, morale, and behavior of people. Schemes that require *realistic* and *feasible* changes in behavior, that incorporate incentives for change are more likely to be successful.

7. In the long run, successful resource reallocation requires information (often comparative information), and supporting analysis. If reallocation is to be based on quantitative analysis, then there must be the technical capability and resources to do so. This can constitute a nontrivial expense.

8. A perfect system cannot be designed. Thus, building in the means for monitoring the reallocation process, for evaluating the results, and for adapting the process are important.

Resource reallocation has strong potential as a managerial response to decline and to opportunity. Whether it will be a stopgap or a positive tool for academic and financial planning is determined in each new manifestation.

References

Cheit, E. F. *The New Depression in Higher Education.* New York: McGraw-Hill, 1971.
Cyert, R. M. *The Management of Nonprofit Organizations.* Lexington, Mass.: Heath, 1975.
Levine, C. H. (Ed.). "Organizational Decline and Cutback Management: A Symposium." *Public Administration Review,* 1978, *38* (4, entire issue).
Mortimer, K. P., and Tierney, M. L. *The Three R's of the Eighties: Reduction, Reallocation, and Retrenchment.* AAHE-ERIC/Higher Education Research Report, No. 4. Washington, D.C.: American Association for Higher Education, 1979.
Priority Fund. Unpublished paper. Ann Arbor: University of Michigan, 1977.
Robl, R. M., Karman, T. A., and Boggs, J. H. "Quality and Vitality Through Reallocation: A Case Study." *Planning for Higher Education,* 1976, *5* (5).
Resource Planning and Excellence. Unpublished paper. Ann Arbor: University of Michigan, 1978.
Shapiro, H. T. "Resource Planning and Flexibility." *Business Officer,* September 1978, pp. 20-23.

R. Sue Mims is director of the Office of Academic Planning and Analysis at the University of Michigan at Ann Arbor.

Attempts to plan or budget without considering the behavioral effects of existing or proposed incentives will produce unintended, and possibly undesirable, results.

The Roles of Incentives in Academic Planning

Stephen A. Hoenack
David J. Berg

Incentives are important influences on behavior in any productive enterprise, public or private, and these influences exist whether or not they are established deliberately by planners. In particular, one cannot choose between an academic planning or budgeting system that has or does not have incentives; there is only the choice of whether to modify incentives. Attempts to plan or budget without considering the behavioral effects of existing incentives or of proposed changes in incentives will result in outcomes that are unintended and often undesirable. Our purposes are to examine the roles of incentives in academic decision making, to suggest potential uses of incentives in academic decision making, and to propose research projects which promise to increase our understanding of desirable uses of incentives in academic planning.

The chapter is organized as follows: The first major section analyzes institutional incentives in terms of the constrained maximization behavior of academic and other personnel. The feasibility of formulating institutional goals and using them as a basis for academic planning is discussed. A definition of incentive is derived, and the importance of basing judgments about the likely effects of potential incentives on the results of existing incentives is explained. "Overall" and "specific" incentives are distinguished. It is suggested that the issue of institutional "fiscal distress" could be most usefully approached behaviorally by considering the incentives faced by academic personnel. The second major section provides a brief overview of existing research on incentives relevant to academic planning; however, our main focus in this discussion is on the major needs for further research. The third major section proposes four research projects that would fill important gaps in our understanding of incentives and planning in institutions of higher education.

Individual Constrained Maximization Behavior—
Implications for Planning

The concept of decentralized incentives is founded on the assumption that individuals base their actions largely on their own self-interest. An individual's self-interested behavior is governed by his or her objectives and the constraints facing him or her; an individual will attempt to maximize achievement of personal objectives subject to the limits imposed by resources available and rules imposed.

An individual's objectives may be expected to be very complex. However, we shall take as given three characteristics of individual objectives: (1) In determining their own objectives, individuals ordinarily give only limited weight, if any, to the objectives of other individuals. For example, the welfare of other faculty members or of students is not in itself a major motivating force in the behavior of an individual faculty member. Exceptions to this assumption are most likely when the individuals are part of the same immediate family. (2) If an individual cannot achieve all of his objectives, he will usually be willing to trade the achievement of one objective for the achievement of another. That is, an increased satisfaction of one objective may compensate for decreased satisfaction or nonsatisfaction of another. (3) Statements of objectives for a group of individuals cannot generally be derived strictly from the objectives of the individuals within the group when the resources to be used for an increase in one individual's satisfaction are (or are perceived to be) at the expense of a decrease in another individual's satisfaction.

The first two characteristics above are assumptions about individuals' utility functions which are often used in economic analysis. See, for example, Stigler (1966) or Watson (1972). The third characteristic is established by Arrow (1950) under a specific set of assumptions. A considerable body of research has subsequently analyzed the implications of assumptions different than those employed by Arrow. A brief review of this research is provided by Mueller (1976).

These characteristics have implications for planning that can be usefully discussed before we consider the nature of constraints on the achievement of objectives. Since individuals' objectives are mostly independent, a faculty member's pursuit of personal objectives will not necessarily achieve any other faculty member's objectives or the objectives of students or other constituencies of a university. For example, an individual faculty member will not typically take as his or her own the goals of a planning committee that are derived from someone else's objectives. The second characteristic, however, suggests that individuals can be led to cooperate in the achievement of another's objectives at the expense of one of their own if, in return, they are able to increase the satisfaction of one or more other objectives. In particular, it may be possible to alter the constraints facing an individual in such a way as to induce him or her to take actions in his or her own interest which in turn increase achievement of the objectives of other individuals.

The third, nonaggregative characteristic implies that a group of individuals, such as an academic planning committee, cannot generally derive a statement of mutual objectives from the objectives of individuals unless one of the following holds: (1) the objectives of one individual are allowed to dictate the importance of the objectives of each individual member of the group; or (2) a set of objectives is imposed on the group. When neither of these conditions holds, group objectives can in general be strictly derived from an aggregation of individual objectives only if they pertain to issues that are unimportant to all but one of the individuals or about which all of these individuals are in agreement.

It should be noted, however, that the second characteristic of an individual's objectives implies that a member of a committee might be induced to endorse an objective other than his own, even at the expense of achieving one of his own objectives. Thus, when there is disagreement, the receipt of compensation by individual committee members to endorse some set of objectives other than their own may make it possible for a committee to achieve a statement of objectives which, however, would not be strictly derived from individual objectives. (Such a statement of objectives would represent a violation of one of Arrow's [1950] assumptions—that pertaining to the irrelevance of independent alternatives.) Members of a committee can compensate each other by exchanging support for each other's objectives. Also, if a party wishing to influence a committee has authority over the resources available to individuals on the committee, compensation can consist of actual or implied commitments of these resources. If feasible, achieving a statement of objectives via compensation is costly in terms of time and other resources. Whether committee members and others are willing to bear these costs depends on perceptions of individually received benefits from the presence of such a statement.

If an institution attempts to use a committee to formulate detailed objectives for institutional planning, the three characteristics of individual objectives imply the following: either the resulting statement of objectives will pertain only to issues for which there is unanimity or which are important to a single member, or the statement will represent exchanges among individual members of the committee and any individuals outside the committee who compensate members of the committee. In the former case, the statement pertains only to limited areas of activity within the institution. In the latter case, the statement pertains to some of the objectives of those involved in the exchanges; these cannot be regarded as representative of all objectives, and particularly not those of individuals not involved in the exchanges. We conclude, therefore, that attempts should not be made to base institutional planning on formulations of detailed objectives. Instead, institutional planning should serve a small number of general objectives which pertain strictly to the institution's overall welfare, as indicated in the quality of the institution's academic programs and efficiency of its resource allocation. Within the concept of efficiency we include flexibility of the institution's programs to serve demands of clienteles.

Given the set of objectives whose achievement depends on the behavior of others than those who hold the objectives, appropriate alteration of constraints on the relevant individuals must take place if the objectives are to be achieved. The costs of altering these incentives are a part of the costs of achieving the objectives and should be taken into account in determining whether achieving the objectives is worthwhile. The appropriate alteration of the incentives for an individual requires an examination of the constraints facing him or her and his or her behavior in relation to these constraints.

The constraints facing an individual consist of the resources available and the terms on which they are available. For a faculty member, for example, the constraints are personal knowledge and abilities and the terms of employment. The terms of employment include job assignments, resources made available to the faculty member, and the reward and penalty structure. Resources made available include such things as equipment, space, laboratory and computer support, and assistants. The reward and penalty structure includes the approval or disapproval of colleagues and superiors and the availability of resources to be used by the faculty member to achieve his own objectives, as well as monetary and fringe benefit compensation. Also, the set of monetary or nonmonetary penalties and rewards may relate to some, but not necessarily to all, resources made available or to every aspect of the faculty member's performance in each job assignment. In a general sense these penalties and rewards connect the individuals' actions in performing their job with the achievement of their own objectives.

Penalties and rewards may attach separately to different aspects of the individual's performance with varying degrees of detail or may relate more generally to overall productivity as measured by one's total contribution in relation to all of the resources used. Consider, for example, a faculty member engaged in both research and instruction where the production of each is dependent on the monetary or nonmonetary penalties or rewards for each. There are a number of possibilities. (1) Separate penalties or rewards may attach to the performance of research and to instruction as well as to the resources used in the performance of each. (2) It is possible that only one of these contributions or only some of the resources used by the faculty member may be given separate penalties or rewards. (3) Penalties or rewards may pertain generally to the total value of research or instruction performed in relation to the total value of resources used for research or instruction. (4) They may pertain only to particular aspects of these outcomes or particular uses of the resources which lead to these outcomes.

The incentives for an individual are defined to be the set of monetary or nonmonetary penalties or rewards within the constraints facing the individual, which link the achievement of a person's objectives with his or her actions. We now use the term incentive in only this specialized sense. The nature and completeness of incentives depend on the institutional setting and the individual's own bargaining strengths. Whether the incentives that face an individual are monetary depends, in part, on whether there is an organized market in which buyers are willing to pay for each of his or her actions. If there is no market for some of the individual's contributions or for resources used by him, there may not be discrete monetary or nonmonetary incentives established for each. Also existing incentives may be implied within broader incentives if incentives pertain to overall productivity.

Among factors that enter into determination of the incentives facing an individual within an organization are the interests of those who have authority to establish the incentives, the costs of establishing them, the costs of measuring and evaluating performance and uses of resources, and traditions related to the individual's occupation. All of these factors influence the nature of the incentives faced by the individual, including whether or not they encompass the individual's overall contribution to the tasks in which the person is engaged in relation to the resources he or she uses. For example, incentives for instructional activity will be stronger where state support is a large proportion of total institutional support and closely follows teaching workloads. If those who control salary and promotion criteria have a strong interest in research, incentives directed toward research activity will be correspondingly strong. As another example, since each faculty member contributes in only a small way to a student's learning, and this learning and the contribution are difficult and costly to measure, a faculty member does not ordinarily have incentives for this overall contribution in relation to the resources used; his incentives for instruction relate only to particular aspects of this contribution and do so inaccurately.

Thus, individuals acting in their own self-interest maximize the achievement of their individual objectives subject to the constraints—including the incentives built into those constraints—which face them. We refer to this behavior as constrained maximization. We now consider two constrained maximization situations and the relevance of each to planning. First consider the case in which the incentives facing an individual are those which currently exist. Do these incentives lead the faculty member, staff employee, or student to take actions that are beneficial to the college or university, or are the existing incentives harmful in particular respects? For example, the frequently discussed issue of "fiscal distress" in colleges and universities can be considered from the perspective of the incentives facing faculty and other staff. To what extent do existing incentives lead staff to pursue activities that impose costs on the institution considerably in excess of what external clienteles are willing to pay? Of course, any high quality institution seeks to encourage such activities when its prestige and the excellence of its research and instruction are strongly enhanced as a result. However, knowledge about existing incentives can help an institution to correct situations where activities are being elicited that are especially costly in relation to what paying clienteles are willing to support, when these activities enhance the institution's reputation and quality modestly or not at all.

The second constrained maximization case is that in which the incentives faced by an individual are altered by a change in policy. If a policy change does not alter the objectives of individuals, its effects, if any, must come through altering the constraints facing them—tasks assigned, resources made available, or incentives. If a change in policy used to implement a plan is to have desirable effects for an institution, it must alter the constraints in such a way that new constrained maximizations take place which in turn result in desired individual actions under the institutional plan. Thus if a new policy ignores the constrained maximizations of the individuals affected by the policy, the policy will lead to desirable changes in behavior only coincidentally. An even more serious problem is the possibility that undesired changes in behavior may result from a failure to consider the constrained maximizations of affected individuals. Well-intentioned planning may, for instance, make an institution's fiscal distress worse by creating incentives for costly activities for which the institution is not adequately rewarded.

From the foregoing discussion we conclude that if planning is to be effective, it must take into account the constrained maximization behavior of individuals whose constraints are affected by policies associated with the plan. Now we must consider whether this can be done and, if it can, the costs of doing so.

Since each individual's objectives are probably unique, making inferences about them may not be feasible and, if feasible, may be very costly. If planners are to be informed about each individual's area of expertise and production technology, costly duplication of technical expertise may be necessary. Individuals will furnish it only insofar as doing so will further their self-interest. This problem can be avoided only when planners adhere to particular criteria for allowable types of policies.

At this point it is useful to distinguish between *overall incentives* and *specific incentives*. This distinction is based on the concepts of *overall replacement responsibility* and *specific responsibility* assigned to employees in Hoenack (forthcoming). The following discussion provides only a very brief summary of some of the characteristics of overall and specific incentives and is necessarily superficial. Also, the following discussion does not deal with differential effects on demands for information or other resource allocation behavior resulting from the choice between overall and specific incentives.

An overall incentive system holds an individual or a group of individuals (such as an academic department) responsible for total outcomes in relation to all of the resources used. In contrast, a specific incentive pertains to only one aspect of the outcomes produced by an individual or a group or only to particular uses of resources while ignoring outcomes.

Examples of specific incentives are establishing work rules for a faculty member such as requiring physical presence at particular times, monitoring compliance, and providing resources which make tasks desired of the faculty member more agreeable to him or her. Another example of a specific incentive is enforcing a requirement of particular levels of output with rewards or penalties independent of the resources used to produce outputs. Such incentives motivate behavior specifically in regard to the particular activities to which the incentives pertain; the faculty member is led to attend to these aspects of his job rather than being concerned with overall efficiency in using resources to produce desired outcomes. It would be extremely costly to apply specific incentives to every resource in exactly the manner which elicits desirable uses of all resources. For this reason, specific incentives usually apply unevenly and lead to inefficient resource allocation.

An overall incentive system requires that the individual or group be permitted to retain the use of all or a significant part of the "profit" represented by the excess of output values over the value of resources used. (Hypotheses about the causal determinants of the size of an individual's budget in relation to the value of his output are derived in Hoenack [forthcoming].) This profit need not be a financial measure. An example of overall incentives with a measured financial profit is the earmarking of income generated by a college for that college's use and charging the college for the resources used by it and the right to retain a substantial portion of any surplus generated from one fiscal period to the next. The duty to take actions to cure deficits is also part of such an overall incentive. Thus if the college can satisfactorily perform its expected instructional and service functions at a profit, the profit can be used to enhance available resources for scholarship, for example. In this case, the individual or group's share of profit could be represented by personally received pecuniary income, but the profit retention could be restricted to the individual or group's capability to increase activities important to them. That is, the profit could be used to enhance salaries but might alternatively be restricted to be used to increase scholarly opportunity, public service opportunity, or even leisure.

An example of overall incentives without a measured financial profit is the case where, in return for a given budget, a college is required to perform a particular set of instructional tasks. If the college can perform these tasks with less than this budget, the remaining budget represents a profit. While this profit is not a known financial quantity, it is nonetheless a residual which can be of benefit to the college. If faculty attach value to the resources that can be purchased with this profit, a similar motivational effect occurs as if the profit were measured. That is, if, for example, faculty attach value to additional scholarly opportunity achievable with their budgets after meeting the instructional obligations on which their budgets are based, they will be motivated by the unmeasured profit.

Whether or not there is a measured financial profit, when an individual or group has an opportunity to retain profit, there is an incentive to use all the resources available to them efficiently (their funds, space, available staff time, and the like), because any inefficient use reduces profit. In effect, the incentive for the individual or group results in the same behavior as if the planner had gone to the expense of establishing elaborate goals and appropriate specific objectives for each activity and incentives in regard to the use of each resource. The planner need not be concerned with the individual's or the group's specific activities provided that output reaches a prescribed level consistent with the budget. Planning can be focused instead on the appropriate levels of output and budget. Thus, an overall incentive system has the potential to be relatively more economical in terms of costs of information.

Unfortunately, overall incentive systems that are accurately based on values of outputs and inputs may still be uneconomical if it is costly to assign valuations to outputs and inputs of an individual or group. In higher education the valuation of outputs is the most difficult problem. Basing budgets on convenient instructional output measures to the exclusion of measures of instructional and research quality (which are extremely difficult to define or evaluate) creates incentives to increase what is measured, perhaps at the expense of what is not measured. However, even if the research and instruction of a faculty member or a department could be readily evaluated, it might be costly to identify and assign values to those resources used by an individual or group within an organization which are beyond the formally budgeted and directly charged resource costs. For example, the accurate allocation of faculty effort between one output, for which there is an overall incentive, and another output, for which there is not an overall incentive, may be extremely costly or infeasible. Another possible problem with overall incentives is the possibility that the bargaining power of some individuals or groups within the organization may enable them to demand and receive considerably higher resource levels in relation to the value of the associated output than they would receive under specific incentives.

One means by which to assign values to the outputs of an individual or group is to allow clienteles to have a direct influence on budgets if they directly receive the outputs. Aside from avoiding costs of measuring and assigning values, there are a number of circumstances which enhance the desirability of this means of measuring and attaching values to outputs. In one circumstance clienteles make informed choices and have access to competing suppliers. In another circumstance rewards are also provided by the organization for those valuable outputs which are not valued by clients, but which are nonetheless important to the organization (basic research, for example). One important advantage of allowing clienteles to influence budgets is that it ensures that decision makers within the organization are not insulated from the dependence of the organization's long-run welfare on the clienteles.

With specific incentives, the economies in information brought about by the individual or group's profit incentive are lost. Further, such incentives can be counterproductive when introduced in the absence of detailed information about productivity. The availability of information regarding particular uses of resources may lead to the introduction of incentives which encourage these uses of resources at the expense of other and more desirable activities for which sufficient information to formulate and introduce encouraging incentives is unobtainable. Alternatively, the use of specific incentives could require planners to obtain enormously costly information in order to establish appropriate incentives for all activities, thus avoiding the counterproductive effects of introducing individual incentives out of context.

While specific incentives can have counterproductive effects if planners fail to obtain complete and detailed information about the actions and productivity of the individuals or groups to which they are applied, there are two conditions under which much less of this information is required for the introduction of specific incentives. One condition is that a specific incentive applies relatively uniformly to a large number of individuals or groups within an organization. The second condition is that a specific incentive directly or indirectly affects particular outputs and particular resource uses but not others. (This condition would result from what is referred to in economics literature as the "separability" of objective functions and production functions on which individuals' constrained maximizations are based, or from offsetting effects within these functions.) In this case the planner would need to possess information about only a particular subset of actions and productivities to evaluate the incentive. The existence of this condition, combined with the condition that all individuals and groups respond in a similar way to the incentive, could substantially reduce the cost of information required to evaluate specific incentives.

As an example, it may be reasonable to assume a relatively uniform and predictable response of faculty to a new incentive for introducing a continuing education program or a sponsored research project. Further, it may be reasonable to assume that the new incentive would draw faculty efforts away from some activities, such as research or instruction, but not from others. If such assumptions are valid, the costs of evaluating the introduction of specific incentives could be substantially reduced.

To what types of policies should planners direct their attention? Whenever possible, overall incentives should be introduced to hold faculty or departments responsible for the values of all the outputs for which there is demand when they are expected to be responsive to such demand in relation to the value of the resources used by them. In this way the individual or group has the equivalent of a profit motive to economize without the planner needing detailed and costly information about these activities. Only in particular circumstances should policies be used which introduce specific incentives lacking this profit motive. Such circumstances include those where incentives are expected to affect only limited areas of behavior or where they affect different individuals or groups relatively uniformly; in these circumstances the effects of incentives, including possible counterproductive effects, can be predicted relatively economically. Planners should strenuously avoid evaluating and discourage implementing policies that do not meet these criteria. In particular, policies should not be implemented whose effects are so costly to assess that the results could be known only after the policy was implemented, if at all.

Earlier we spoke of the effects of incentives on an organization's supply of the outputs of the individuals and groups working within it. Of equal importance to planning is the demand for these outputs. We have already briefly considered demand in connection with the possibility that perverse incentives may produce institutional fiscal distress by encouraging outputs that are more costly to produce than clienteles are willing to pay. Planners, however, should be generally concerned with the demand for those outputs whose supply is affected by existing or proposed incentives within a policy. For example, a policy within a college or university may include incentives that increase the supply of instruction or the supply of research activity. For instruction, what are the related student demands? If the increased supply of instruction caters to nontraditional age groups, do the enrollment demands of these groups differ from those of the traditional age groups? If the institution is publicly financed, what are the legislative demands for its instructional activities?

Regarding research, we must distinguish basic from applied research. Applied research provides a direct benefit to a clientele who in turn may be willing to pay for it. The benefits of basic research are so diffused that no one, not even individual governmental agencies, will pay for it as an individually received benefit, though the state or federal governments may support it as a collective benefit to society at large. In considering incentives to increase the supply of applied research, planners should be concerned with demands, whether from federal or state governments or from private sources. Because of the importance of basic research to society at large as well as its effects on the quality of a higher education institution, planners should be very concerned with funding for this research. One possible internal source is the "profit" resulting from increased efficiency under overall incentives; most universities already force students and governments to share the cost of basic research as a profit from instruction. It is important for universities of high quality that incentives encouraging instruction do not do so at the expense of the basic research that maintains their quality. On the other hand, care should be taken to distinguish basic research from applied research for which there is little or no demand.

Brief Overview of Existing Research—
Suggestions for Further Research

Space limitations require that the overview and discussion of existing research be extremely brief. For further detail the reader may consult the references.

For colleges and universities, a number of authors have proposed budgeting systems that create overall incentives by tying the incomes of academic units to their enrollments, charging them for the resources they use, and allowing them to retain all or part of the surplus or to make adjustments in subsequent budget proposals to recover all or part of their losses. (See Dunworth and Cook, 1976; Hoenack, 1977; Hoenack and Norman, 1974; Layard and Jackman, 1973; and University of Pennsylvania, 1973. Important theoretical discussions which are particularly interesting in the evaluation of a responsibility budgeting system are provided by Bear, 1974, Cootner, 1974, Daniere, 1964, and Reder, 1974.) We refer to these proposals as "responsibility budgeting systems." A number of private institutions have actually implemented responsibility budgeting systems, and published reports explore the problems experienced in providing appropriate information to academic units under such a system at the University of Pennsylvania (see Strauss, 1975; Strauss and Salamon, 1979; and Zemsky, Porter and Oedel, 1978).

A number of variants on responsibility budgeting systems have been proposed or exist in practice. The level at which the cost or responsibility center is established may vary (at the level of a college within a university, for example, or at a level of an academic department within a college). There may be an explicit policy of expecting some units to provide a degree of subsidy to other units. Some part of an institution, such as lower division or liberal arts college instruction, may be excluded from responsibility budgeting.

One of the proposed systems includes a simulation of costs, revenues, and surplus (referred to as *discretionary funds*) of a responsibility budgeting system proposed for the University of Minnesota. (See Hoenack, 1977; this study also analyzes issues in implementing a responsibility budgeting system in a public institution and explores the roles of a university's administration under such a system.) Such a simulation requires explicit incorporation of actual instructional demand into a model of the budgeting system. For a public institution, demand for instructional services as expressed by public subsidy, as well as student demand are incorporated. The resulting simulations show large effects on discretionary funds of both the response of legislative funding to increased enrollments and the response of enrollments to alternative tuition policies. In other words, this study suggests that demand plays a major quantitative role in the evaluation of a responsibility budgeting system.

The authors are not aware of any case in which a responsibility budgeting system has been put into practice in a purely public institution. This raises the question of whether planning and budgeting systems which evaluate and utilize incentives are impractical for public institutions. There seem to be three reasons why the introduction of such systems is more difficult in public than in private institutions. Student demand presently appears to be more easily measurable and predictable than legislative support. Since the latter controls a major portion of the funds available for instruction in public institutions and is comparatively negligible for private institutions, public institutions are far less willing to base policy making on assumptions about legislative behavior than are private institutions. A related but more specific problem is the reluctance of public funding agencies to allow surpluses patently generated by efficiency incentives to remain, at least in large part, within the institution. Without the flexibility, overall incentive systems cannot influence self-interested behavior. Perhaps the most important reason is that a responsibility budgeting system would make explicit the subsidies received by a university's various constituencies. Those constituencies, who would fear loss of their subsidies if identifiable, would be strongly opposed to a responsibility budgeting system for this reason.

In spite of the greater difficulty, the possibility of introducing overall incentive systems within public institutions deserves serious consideration. Some public institutions are already able to retain efficiency surpluses in an accounting sense,* although without more information about legislative demand behavior it is a question whether they

---

*Information on this point is closely guarded. The authors are aware of one public university which has a tacit agreement with state authorities that allows it to keep funds associated with positions which can be abolished as they become vacant and to

have been recovered by reducing a subsequent appropriation. Above all, governors, legislatures, and coordinating boards may become convinced that the more flexible approach to budgeting needed for overall incentives in the academic planning of public insitutions can produce more efficiency and more responsiveness to clienteles. The support of the additional clienteles served as a result of this responsiveness should outweigh the loss of support of those constituencies who would lose their subsidies under a responsibility budgeting system.

All authors of proposed responsibility budgeting systems as well as administrators of existing responsibility budgeting systems emphasize the difficulty of introducing incentives for quality of instruction into payments to academic units. They also cite the issue of supply of instruction in response to incentives, particularly in regard to continuing education programs for age groups other than the traditional clienteles of higher education. Research on both of these topics could be especially important in the evaluation of responsibility budgeting systems.

A recent proposal at Yale University is an important step in the direction of including research incentives within responsibility budgeting systems (see Schultz and others, 1978). Under this proposal academic departments would directly receive a large portion of the university's indirect cost recoveries and would be directly charged for some of the institutional services associated with sponsored research which are currently provided without direct charges. Note that implementing such a mechanism would require more information than usually exists about the exact incidence within a university of costs associated with sponsored research. The nature of indirect cost accounting systems on which overhead charges are based suggests that the exact incidence has usually not been determined. Under a related mechanism proposed at Yale, an internal accounting system for all faculty research time (not just sponsored research time) would be introduced so that a larger fraction of faculty research time would be subject to peer review and competition on the basis of the merit of the research proposals of individual faculty members. This mechanism would establish larger "base" teaching loads combined with a correspondingly larger pool of released time for research activity. Faculty members would apply to this pool for released time, and awards from the pool would be based on peer review of the proposals.

---

use such funds to enhance salaries and fringe benefits. Authorities at that university did not want the scheme to be specifically cited. This illustrates the touchiness of such arrangements in the public sector, notwithstanding the fact that both the school and the state are probably benefiting from the overall incentive.

These proposed mechanisms deserve serious consideration. The first proposal could create additional incentives for faculty to apply for research grants and for academic departments to provide faculty with released time and other resources for the preparation of external proposals. It also, however, runs one of the risks cited above for institutions dependent on governmental behavior if an observable surplus would result. Past experience would suggest that the federal government might attempt to recover not merely a part, but all of that surplus. If this occurs, obviously much of the advantage of the incentive is lost for both buyer and seller.

The second proposal could create several desirable incentives. One would relate to the quality of basic research. Introducing competition for released time based on peer review would result in the relatively more talented scholars receiving relatively more released time for research. Also individual scholars would have opportunities to receive criticism of their ideas in their early stages. A further desirable incentive would be to encourage faculty doing applied research to seek sponsored research funding. Because released time for nonsponsored research would be scarce and subject to competition, those performing the review process would have an incentive to economize on this released time by encouraging those faculty whose proposals could potentially be externally funded to seek such funding. Nerlove (1971) presents a number of interesting hypotheses about the effects of such mechanisms on both research and teaching activities; under certain circumstances larger quantities of both activities could be the result.

A number of proposals have been made for incentives within higher education which are not placed in the context of other incentives for faculty and do not allow for profits. Thus these proposals represent specific incentives and should be evaluated further, either in the context of a responsibility budgeting system or theoretical work on their potential effects on faculty behavior, including activities other than those to which the incentives directly apply. Some of these proposals, nonetheless, are of considerable interest. (See Breneman, 1971, for a number of such proposals and commentary about them by researchers and administrators.) Becker's theoretical work (1975; 1979) about the behavior of individual academic personnel derives testable hypotheses about the behavioral effects of a number of possible specific incentives. One of these hypotheses is that specific incentives directed to teaching will increase teaching quality. (See also the papers within Lewis and Becker, 1979, for insights into individual faculty behavior which could lead to further theoretical work on the effects of specific incentives.)

Except for Breneman's (1970) important analysis of the instructionally related incentives implicit in the University of California's budget system, we know of no research that makes inferences about the behavioral effects of existing incentives in higher education institutions. As a result, there is at present little empirical basis for understanding the causes or remedies of institutional "fiscal distress."

In regard to demand for the activities that would be affected by incentives, considerable research on the enrollment demand of students has already been done. These studies provide estimates of the effects of tuition, labor market variables, and other influences on students' enrollment choices. These estimates could be useful in evaluating the behavioral effects of incentives to increase enrollments. Published surveys of existing research on enrollment demand include Jackson and Weathersby (1973), Radner and Miller (1975), and Weinschrott (1977). Hoenack and Weiler (1979) present an institutional enrollment forecasting model. This model includes estimated equations of enrollment demand which incorporate tuition, labor markets, and other variables which influence demand, and estimated equations which are used to forecast values of the labor market variables which influence demand. These estimated equations permit enrollment forecasts conditional on assumed values of the variables that influence enrollment demand and calculations of the statistical confidence intervals around enrollment forecasts. Of particular interest is a study by Bishop and Van Dyk (1977) of the determinants of continuing education enrollments. Much less research has been done on the enrollment, research, and public service demands of legislatures and private donors.

The existing research on legislative demand is based largely on the "median voter model." Because this model is based on the assumption that the citizen with median preferences about higher education subsidies determines legislative funding, it cannot be counted upon to take into account the pressures on legislators by the direct beneficiaries of educational subsidies. (See Bergstrom and Goodman, 1973; Borcherding and Deacon, 1972. A particularly interesting analysis of legislative demand is provided by Clotfelter, 1976. This study goes beyond the "median voter model" but provides no direct inference within the equation for legislative demand about the behavior of beneficiaries of educational subsidies.) Some very useful research has been performed related to the demand of private donors (Feldstein, 1975; Reece, 1979) but there exists virtually no information on governmental and other demand for faculty research activities.

Based on the existing research related to incentives in colleges and universities, we draw the following conclusions about the needs for further research:

1. There is a need for research on the response of faculty to incentives aimed at increasing the supply of instruction to nontra-

ditional clienteles under a responsibility budgeting system. The quality of this supply response and its effects on the quality of performance of other activities should receive particular scrutiny. Specifically, what conditions can ensure high academic quality when an institution creates incentives for an increased supply of instruction to nontraditional clienteles?

2. The incentives implicit in existing institutional planning and budgeting systems should be the subject of future empirical investigation. The results of such research could do much to add behavioral content to discussions of institutional "fiscal distress" and the design of policies in response to it. Studies of "indicators" of fiscal distress do not necessarily determine causes of fiscal distress and, in particular, may not show how incentives could be altered to alleviate fiscal distress. Clurman (1969) presents a valuable behavioral analysis of fiscal distress resulting from competition between public and private institutions.

3. A key need is better understanding of the response of legislative funding to increases in instruction, research, and public service. It seems reasonable to assume that this funding response is more a function of the incentives of individual legislators to support these insittutional activities than of an institution's skill at lobbying. If so, inferences can be made about those incentives.

4. The incidence of costs of sponsored research activities needs to be better understood. A mechanism that creates incentives for faculty to seek research funds must be based on such an improved understanding of the actual costs of sponsored research activities as they affect particular units within an institution. A byproduct would be an improved basis for negotiating sponsored agreements and the possible development of incentive arrangements that could benefit both the sponsor and the institution under such agreements.

Proposed Research on Incentives in Academic Planning

In the following discussion we propose four research projects to address the needs for further research cited in the previous section. Because of space limitations we present only an outline of the general nature of each project; interested researchers are invited to consult the references and the authors for further methodological detail.

Venture Capital Demonstration Projects for Continuing Education. While colleges and universities have successfully introduced continuing education programs in many professional fields, little is known about the fiscal success or the effects of incentives on academic quality when continuing education programs are established in the traditional academic disciplines. The purpose of the projects proposed here would be to experiment with such programs.

The distinguishing feature of the proposed demonstration projects is that academic departments would receive a combination of grants and loans for the purpose of developing continuing education programs over a year or two, and that these departments would subsequently be permitted to retain for themselves a portion of the tuition revenue from the program. Institutional budgeting rules would be flexibly administered to permit the use of these funds in ways desired by faculty (such as small research grants, additional single-term or sabbatical leaves, salary supplements). In this manner the academic departments involved would be given overall incentives with respect to their continuing education activities, yet these incentives would be specific with respect to all of the departmental activities. The demonstration projects would be carefully monitored by researchers within the parent institution to determine quickly when problems occur and make inferences about the behavioral effects of the incentives. Such inferences should pertain not only to the department's production of continuing education but also to the effects on supply and quality of other departmental activities. (The proposed venture capital demonstration projects are discussed in more detail in National Institute of Education, 1978, pp. 9-10.)

An Economic Study of the Determinants of Budgets Within Higher Education Institutions. The purpose of this study would be to make inferences about the incentives on faculty implicit in the determination of college and university budgets. Thus it would be possible to consider whether the presence of certain kinds of incentives is associated with the experience of "fiscal distress." Specifically, incentives might be identified which encourage activities that cost more than external clienteles are willing to pay and are not justified by their effects on the institution's quality and prestige. If such undesirable incentives are discovered, the study could also suggest appropriate alterations in policy.

The proposed study would involve estimating a simultaneous system of equations for (1) demand for departmental activities in which departmental budgets are determined by departmental activities, including enrollments considered within various cost categories, sponsored research, or other research activities; and (2) the supply of departmental activities as a function of budgets.* Both cross-section

---

*Two pioneering studies of incentives within the determination of institutional budgets are Breneman (1970) and Pfeffer and Salancik (1974). Breneman's study addresses incentives affecting time to degree completion, while the Pfeffer and Salancik study addresses the relative effects on departmental budgets of departmental outputs

data for different departments and time series data for each department would be used for estimating the equations. An important purpose of the study would be to permit comparison of the effects of the level of various categories of enrollments on departmental budgets with the funding received by the institution (including legislative funding—see below) for each of these categories.

An Econometric Study of the Legislative Demand for the Activities of Colleges and Universities. If institutions of higher education knew more about legislative demand for their activities—the determinants of the propensity to fund institutional initiatives—they could more easily ascertain the most appropriate levels toward which various kinds of activity should be planned and budgeted and thus, the kinds and degrees of incentives needed to bring forth these supplies. The proposed study of legislative demand would differ from previous analyses by explicitly accounting for the benefits and costs of legislative subsidies to voters within interest groups and the corresponding influences of this voter behavior on legislative subsidies. The equations representing legislative demand for higher education would include variables that control for the number of voters who do and do not directly benefit from subsidies to higher education institutions as well as the sizes of these subsidies.

The selection of variables would be guided by a theory of legislative behavior which posits the role of the "marginal interest group voter," when it is costly for voters to be informed about the subsidies received by other voters. (See Chapter Six of Hoenack [forthcoming].) The model of legislative demand would be estimated with cross-section data for each state. For each state, measures would be constructed for the size of its population that directly benefits from educational subsidies (college-going age groups, their parents, sizes of agricultural and industrial and commercial groups which directly benefit from state funded research, sizes of the instructional subsidies in public institutions, and sizes of subsidies to applied research in these institutions.)

Aside from the potential use of this study in academic planning, it is of broader interest in improving understanding of legislative behavior.

(instruction and research) and the political activity (committee memberships) of departmental faculty. The proposed study would expand the scope of both of these studies to determine the effects of as many as possible of the overall incentives acting on departments and is designed to avoid some methodological difficulties present in the Pfeffer and Salancik study. The most important of these methodological difficulties is the failure to incorporate separate equations for demand and supply of departmental activities.

A Study of Sponsored Research Activity Costs Within Higher Education Institutions. We have seen that a mechanism for the creation of incentives for faculty members to seek sponsored research funds should be based on information about the internal incidence of the costs of sponsored research activities. The proposed study would have two parts. First an institution's expenditure data, together with data relating to utilization of space, libraries, equipment, and other resources would be integrated with interviews with selected principal investigators to calculate economic costs of various types of sponsored research activity among and within disciplines. These calculated costs would certainly differ by discipline and type of research from the costs calculated by use of formula allocations for the assessment of indirect costs, even if the total costs calculated by both methods were identical for the entire institution. The purpose is to obtain estimates of actual costs to ensure that incentives to obtain additional sponsored research funds would not result in costs higher than the additional funding unless an explicit decision to pursue that course has been made. (This discussion relates to an assessment of the effects of existing incentives. Assessment of a proposed change in incentives should use marginal rather than average costs insofar as possible.)

The second part of the proposed study would use an econometric model to estimate the effects of sponsored research activity within an academic department on the costs of its instructional activities. This part of the study would require the specification of a model of the determinants of instructional costs at various levels of different departments within the same discipline in different universities which, according to the published ratings, are of roughly comparable quality and alike in certain other organizational characteristics. (A likely source of much of the necessary data is the "credit/enrollment" data which the Association of American Universities Data Exchange has been slowly bringing toward comparability over the past several years, together with certain other public or exchange data from the AAUDE institutions.) One of the major determinants of these costs is almost certainly the level and volume of enrollments. Sponsored research activity of departmental faculty and several other variables are also hypothesized to be important determinants of costs.

The proposed study would avoid some of the problems encountered in the Verry and Davies (1976) study of costs in British Universities which provides estimates of effects of research activity on institutional costs. Most importantly, the proposed study would allow for divergences between marginal and average costs through specification of core faculties and augmentation to core faculties in response to increased enrollments, and, additionally, allow for more precise measurements of research activities.

Summary

Incentives are present in the operations of every college or university. An understanding of them is crucial to the success or failure of academic planning efforts. The lack of attention directed to incentives in most formal planning systems inevitably results in unintended outcomes which are often undesirable. The common approach to formulating through compromise a mission with goals and objectives, and assuming that individuals within the organization will support the achievement of the plans, ignores what is known about self-interested economic behavior and is unlikely to have the intended effects.

There are strategies which have the potential to introduce effective incentives at manageable costs. Such incentives have the potential to help academic institutions avoid fiscal distress and make themselves more flexible in adjusting to changes in the needs and demands of their clienteles. The effects of incentives on behavior within academic institutions deserve much more study than they have received.

References

Arrow, K. J. "A Difficulty in the Concept of Social Welfare." *Journal of Political Economy,* 1950, *58,* 328-346.

Bear, D. V. T. "The University as a Multi-Product Firm." In K. G. Lumsden (Ed.), *Efficiency in Universities: The La Paz Papers.* New York: Elsevier, 1974.

Becker, W. E., Jr. "The University Professor as a Utility Maximizer and Producer of Learning, Research, and Income." *Journal of Human Resources,* 1975, *10,* 107-115.

Becker, W. E., Jr. "Professorial Behavior Given a Stochastic Reward Structure." *American Economic Review,* 1979, *69,* 1010-1017.

Bergstrom, T. C., and Goodman, R. P. "Private Demand for Public Goods." *American Economic Review,* 1973, *63,* 280-296.

Bishop, J., and Van Dyk, J. "Can Adults Be Hooked on College? Some Determinants of Adult College Attendance." *Journal of Higher Education,* 1977, *48,* 39-62.

Borcherding, T. E., And Deacon, R. T. "The Demand for the Services of Non-Federal Government." *American Economic Review,* 1972, *62,* 891-901.

Breneman, D. W. *An Economic Theory of Ph.D. Production: The Case at Berkeley.* Paper P-8, Ford Foundation Research Program in University Administration. Berkeley: University of California, 1970.

Breneman, D. W. *Internal Pricing Within the University—A Conference Report.* Report P-24, Ford Foundation Program for Research in University Administration. Berkeley: University of California, 1971.

Clotfelter, C. T. "Public Spending for Higher Education: An Empirical Test of Two Hypotheses." *Public Finance,* 1976, *31,* 177-195.

Clurman, M. "Does Higher Education Need More Money?" In *The Economics and Financing of Higher Education in the United States.* A compendium of papers submitted to the Joint Economic Committee. Washington, D.C.: U.S. Government Printing Office, 1969.

Cootner, P. H. "Economic Organization in the Modern University." In K. G. Lumsden (Ed.), *Efficiency in Universities: The La Paz Papers.* New York: Elsevier, 1974.

Daniere, A. *Higher Education in the American Economy.* New York: Random House, 1964.

Dunworth, J., and Cook, R. "Budgetary Devolution As an Aid to University Efficiency." *Higher Education,* 1976, *5,* 153-167.

Feldstein, M. "The Income Tax and Charitable Contributions: Part II—The Impact on Religious, Educational, and Other Organizations." *National Tax Journal,* 1975, *28,* 209-226.

Hoenack, S. A. "Direct and Incentive Planning Within a University." *Socio-Economic Planning Sciences,* 1977, *11,* 191-204.

Hoenack, S. A. *Economic Behavior Within Organizations.* London and New York: Cambridge University Press, forthcoming.

Hoenack, S. A., and Norman, A. L. "Incentives and Resource Allocation Within Universities." *Journal of Higher Education,* 1974, *45,* 21-37.

Hoenack, S. A., and Weiler, W. C. "The Demand for Higher Education and Institutional Enrollment Forecasting." *Economic Inquiry,* 1979, *17,* 89-113.

Jackson, G. A., and Weathersby, G. B. "Individual Demand for Higher Education: A Review and Analysis of Recent Empirical Studies." *Journal of Higher Education,* 1973, *46,* 623-652.

Layard, R., and Jackman, R. "University Efficiency and University Finance." In M. Parkin and A. R. Nobay (Eds.), *Essays in Modern Economics.* London: Longman's, 1973.

Lewis, D. R., and Becker, W. E., Jr. *Academic Rewards in Higher Education.* Cambridge, Mass.: Ballinger, 1979.

Mueller, D. C. "Public Choice: A Survey." *Journal of Economic Literature,* 1976, *14,* 395-433.

National Institute of Education. *Finance, Productivity, and Management in Postsecondary Research Topics: Selected Research Topics.* Washington, D.C.: U.S. Government Printing Office, 1978.

Nerlove, M. "On Tuition and the Costs of Higher Education: Prolegomena to a Conceptual Framework." *Journal of Political Economy,* 1972, *80,* 178-218.

Pfeffer, J., and Salancik, G. R. "Organizational Decision Making as Political Process: The Case of a University Budget." *Administrative Science Quarterly,* 1974, *19,* 135-151.

Radner, R., and Miller, L. S. *Demand and Supply in U.S. Higher Education.* New York: McGraw-Hill, 1975.

Reder, M. W. "A Suggestion for Increasing the Efficiency of Universities." In K. G. Lumsden (Ed.), *Efficiency in Universities: The La Paz Papers.* New York: Elsevier, 1974.

Reece, W. S. "New Evidence on Household Behavior." *American Economic Review,* 1979, *69,* 142-151.

Schultz, T. P., and others. *Report of the Committee on the Economic Status of the Faculty of Yale College and the Graduate School.* New Haven, Conn.: Yale University, 1979.

Stigler, G. J. *The Theory of Price.* (3rd ed.) New York: Macmillan, 1966.

Strauss, J. C. "Administrative Information Systems for Planning. Defining the Future." In *Proceedings EDUCOM 1975 Spring Conference.* Princeton, N.J.: EDUCOM, 1975.

Strauss, J. C., and Salamon, L. D. "Using Financial Incentives in Academic Planning and Management." *Business Officer,* 1979, *13,* 14-17.

University of Pennsylvania. *Pennsylvania: One University: Report of the University Development Commission.* Philadelphia: University of Pennsylvania, 1973.

Verry, D., and Davies, B. *University Costs and Outputs.* Amsterdam: Elsevier, 1976.

Watson, D. S. *Price Theory and Its Uses.* (3rd ed.) New York: Houghton Mifflin, 1972.

Weinschrott, D. *Demand for Higher Education in the United States: A Critical Review of the Empirical Literature.* Santa Monica, Calif.: Rand Corporation, 1977.

Zemsky, R., Porter, R., and Oedel, L. P. "Decentralized Planning Responsibility." *Educational Record,* 1978, *59,* 229-253.

Stephen A. Hoenack is director of Management Information Division and professor in the Hubert H. Humphrey Institute of Public Affairs, University of Minnesota.

David J. Berg is director of Management Planning and Information Services, University of Minnesota.

*The conditions facing postsecondary education during the
1980s call for institutional planning styles that are
comprehensive, systematic, public, regular,
and expansive.*

Academic Program Planning Reconsidered

Richard B. Heydinger

The previous four chapters have described four different approaches to academic program planning. The introductory chapter illustrated nine other "styles" by which academic programs are planned. Some of these styles, such as program data, are best described as tools which support program planning. Other styles, such as the formal democratic, are comprehensive processes that build on the theories of organizational development and planning. A number of the styles cited in Chapter One, such as knowledge development or problem focused, would not be considered planning in the context of contemporary usage. Yet the Random House Dictionary says that a plan is any method for thinking out acts and purposes beforehand. Certainly these individually based planning styles, although random and nonsystematic, are methods for charting tomorrow's actions.

Hence, when addressing academic program planning it is important to recognize the vast number of alternative ways in which instructional programs are designed and implemented. Academic leaders and institutional researchers must be cognizant of this variety of planning styles, utilizing the ones which address the issues at hand. To be an effective administrator or sensitive institutional researcher, inherent assumptions and subtle differences which underlie each approach must be recognized. Also, it is important to understand that the planning of academic programs takes place throughout colleges and universities and from many different perspectives. Individual faculty members engage in program planning when they decide which materials to include in a course. Departments, colleges, institutions, and systems all participate in the process which I term *academic program planning*. Also, it must be understood that selected aspects of a number of these styles, although discussed separately in this sourcebook, are combined to make up the planning approach of a college or university. Academic program planning cannot be fully understood until its multiplicity of dimensions is recognized.

This final chapter stands back from this variety of program planning approaches and contrasts them with one another. The author has taken on the role of critic. Just as the license of the movie critic encourages the inclusion of personal bias and philosophy, the author's beliefs come to the fore. I hope that the reader will emerge from this discussion with a greater understanding of academic program planning.

In this concluding chapter each of the four planning approaches described in the previous chapters is reviewed separately. A fifth style, the formal democratic, is also discussed because of its widespread use in education. The chapter concludes with some general comments on academic program planning.

Needs Assessment

As Lenning notes in his chapter, satisfying needs is a theme that underlies much of our educational system and indeed is an integral part of our culture. Thus, it is natural that educational institutions would set out to determine the needs of students, potential employers, and the community when planning an academic program. Yet a major segment of postsecondary education—specifically, four-year colleges and graduate institutions—generally has not conducted formal needs assessments. No doubt, mechanisms such as accrediting agencies and community advisory groups do bring to the campus anecdotal evidence of the need for curricular change. Yet higher education traditionally has remained aloof from the community and its potential students, and has not systematically reached out to determine educational need. The developmental work in needs assessment has taken place in those sectors of education that are most closely tied to the local community—primary and secondary schools and community colleges.

However, with enrollment pressures predicted to grow, many colleges and even some universities are now looking for new segments of the market which they might be able to tap. Needs assessment is offered as a planning tool that can point to fruitful new student markets. Yet it has a more palatable purpose as well. Needs assessment can be used as a retrospective tool to determine the effectiveness of our present educational offerings. For institutions that view their mission as serving the community or society, needs assessment is an essential tool.

This planning approach should be viewed as an "idea generator," an antecedent to program planning. The results of such studies can stimulate the thinking of those responsible for actually planning programs. In this way needs assessment is a support tool for a formal planning process. In using the results from needs assessments, colleges and universities should not lose sight of their fundamental mission. In the 1980s, particularly with smaller institutions, the temptation will be to respond to any unmet need. Colleges and universities must carefully consider society's needs vis-à-vis their individual programmatic resources and philosophical purposes. In the 1980s institutions of higher learning must resist the temptation to respond to each and every market.

In designing and conducting needs assessments, as Lenning points out, there must be a clear recognition of whose needs are being described. In some instances a needs assessment should tap the needs of potential employers; for other purposes program alumni may be the best source of data; yet in many cases potential enrollees may provide the necessary information. Decisions on the best source of needs information should be based on the purposes of the study.

Perhaps the most problematic aspect of designing a needs assessment is distinguishing between "effective demand" and "expressed need" when measuring the potential market for a program. Before offering a program, many institutions want to know whether there will be demand sufficient to support a program offering. Potential students are surveyed and the needs assessment data show a high degree of interest. Yet when the program is offered, few students enroll. Although the *expressed demand* was evident, the *effective demand* (in other words, program enrollment) did not materialize. This issue remains one of the fundamental challenges in using needs assessment data aimed at predicting actual program demand.

As a planning style, needs assessment is a data collection approach that relies on the techniques of social science research including public polling. To ensure validity and reliability, methodologies must be designed which utilize the proven fundamentals of survey research. Yet because such studies are often prohibitively expensive, the institutional researcher must retreat to a refined design. Innovative techniques must be created that will collect valid data yet fall within budgetary and time constraints. Although Lenning mentions a number of innovative approaches for data collection, a great deal more attention must be devoted to work in this area.

Needs assessment will be an increasingly important planning tool in the 1980s. It is free of the decision-making style of the institution and can be used within any organizational structure. As a planning style, it can be used to foster a greater understanding of the community and to narrow the chasms which sometimes seem to separate higher education from the remainder of society. Perhaps most importantly, formal needs assessments are not limited to the planning of academic programs. They can be used as the initial step in planning research activities, tuition plans, or even internal changes in governance mechanisms.

Program Data

Somewhat akin to needs assessment, the program data approach to academic program planning assembles statistics that can be used in support of program planning decisions. Simply assembling data on programs obviously does not constitute program planning. However, creating such a data base can often be a useful first step in moving toward effective program planning. If a desired characteristic of improved planning is a more rational decision-making process, comprehensive data on the current status and historical trends of each program must be available. Such data provide valuable comparative information and are benchmarks against which the effect of planning decisions can be measured. However, neither the development of a data base nor the associated statistical analysis should be interpreted as synonymous with planning.

In contrast to a needs assessment which may point toward new ideas for program planning, program data provides detailed information on the current state of affairs. Detailed data reports on each program, as exemplified by Freeman and Simpson in Chapter Three, may lead to new insights into the operation of the institution. This increased understanding could in turn result in more informed planning decisions. As a support for program planning, the collection of program data should not be expected to expand significantly the horizons of ideas considered by those making planning decisions. Instead, comprehensive program data will ensure that programs are being treated equitably, that planning decisions are consistent with intended priorities, and that decisions are being made on an informed basis.

In order to build and maintain a comprehensive and consistent set of program data, one must have a centralized office of institutional research. This professional staff group should be in the best position to ensure that data elements are consistently defined so that inter-unit comparisons can be made. This office can also assume the responsibility for collecting the data on a regular basis so that trends can be charted.

Some institutional researchers resist the creation of a comprehensive institutional data base, noting that it is "data in search of a question." Instead, they want only to respond to pressing institutional matters with specific research studies. Although such studies can fill an important institutional need, comprehensive longitudinal program data is a necessity in planning and administering any organization, particularly those as complex as today's colleges and universities.

A program data approach to planning builds on the existing structure of the institution. It is an *ex post facto,* detailed look at each program on which future decisions can be built. As described in this volume, this planning approach is designed by the central administration, and maintenance of the data base is an administrative staff function. Yet program data is a *tool* of academic program planning. It does not assume any particular style of decision making. It can augment both highly decentralized or highly centralized planning approaches. For example, comparable program data can be distributed to all departments and colleges. In turn, planning at each of these levels can be informed by these statistics. If both central administration and the academic units have the same data available (and all parties generally agree on its validity), the debate can focus on major educational issues rather than specific questions of program status or data accuracy. Obviously this promotes more effective planning. Although the compilation of program data does not guarantee effective planning, it is a necessary building block for any college or university in both planning and day-to-day decision making. Without it there is no check for ascertaining whether one's perceptions are supported by objective evidence.

Retrenchment and Reallocation

Contemporary higher education literature is replete with references to "R&R," so much so that the phrase has become hackneyed and lost any vitality it may have had. Yet a carefully designed retrenchment and reallocation procedure can be a potentially valuable planning and budgeting tool. Some people would argue that R&R is only a budgeting tool and should not be considered as an approach to academic program planning. Yet, as Mims points out in Chapter Four, R&R can play an important role in institutions that have other forms of effective long-range planning, for it can provide an effective link between budgeting and planning. In Chapter Three, Simpson and Freeman describe Michigan State's development of an R&R approach that is supported by the use of comprehensive program data and the EDUCOM Financial Planning Model to aid in forecasting how much retrenchment and reallocation ought to take place. Retrenchment and reallocation strategies must be viewed as a tool that can bring resource allocation decisions into line with academic program planning.

In discussing retrenchment and reallocation it is important to distinguish the one-time budgetary procedure from the ongoing, multiyear process. The former is a quick budget "fix" which sets out to bring resource allocation into line with program priorities. Although perhaps it could be argued that it is a planning approach, it typically views the future only in terms of the upcoming budget cycle. The multiyear process offers a much greater potential for acting on the institution's long-range visions than does R&R. Across a number of iterations the institution can wittingly move funds from one program to another, thus strategically moving toward its vision of the future.

If retrenchment and reallocation is to be effective in linking academic priorities with resource decisions, a clear set of institutional program priorities must be articulated a priori. Without this the R&R, the decision-making process at many institutions will remain a round of budgetary horse trading between academic and fiscal officers which lacks an articulated view of the institution's future. With a clear set of academic priorities, an institution can gradually and effectively shift its educational and research outcomes through a multiyear retrenchment and reallocation process.

Usually the impetus for introducing a retrenchment and reallocation process is an impending budgetary crisis. Yet R&R is an appropriate tool for use in periods of growth. Just as the growing plant thrives and takes shape with pruning, so might higher education programs. Perhaps postsecondary education would not be so alarmed over its future if during the halcyon days of the 1960s it had continually been pruning its academic programs through a process of retrenchment and reallocation. Effective academic administrators and program planners must see the importance of introducing such countervailing measures.

A retrenchment and reallocation approach to academic program planning can be designed as a decentralized approach to decision making. For example, at the University of Michigan each unit is asked annually to give up 1 percent of its budget. Which degree programs to cut back are decisions that can be made at the departmental or collegiate level. Similarly, deciding on which existing programs to expand or which new programs to develop may be done at the level of the individual unit. Obviously final decisions rest with central decision-making authorities; but the R&R process, if properly designed, can be consistent with the norms of academic governance essential to effective academic planning.

As Mims points out, R&R procedures are often established as a parallel process to the traditional resource acquisition and allocation mechanism. If this is the case, the institution is not correcting the situation that led to the necessity for an R&R process. Instead, R&R has become a temporary fix, used to correct some other imbalance in the institution.

This style of program planning offers the potential for effective planning but certainly does not ensure it. R&R will *not* encourage individual faculty to think more futuristically. Its influence may be felt solely through the preparation of budget requests and the awarding of funds. Any increase in the faculty member or department's awareness of long-range planning issues will come about when academic priorities are discussed. If an R&R process is an essential component of a planning process, then it has this potential. If it is used narrowly as a budgeting tool, it will not necessarily produce any more effective planning than currently exists.

Incentive Planning

To understand incentive planning it is best to begin the discussion with an examination of the assumptions on which this planning style is based. Advocates of incentive planning argue persuasively that these assumptions apply to any organization, regardless of the planning approach utilized. And, as shall be discussed later, ignoring these fundamental conditions will undermine the effectiveness of any planning approach.

There are three fundamental assumptions. First, there is a series of incentives to which all of us respond. Although these incentives may not be immediately obvious and most likely will differ somewhat for each person, our behavior is in large measure determined by our own incentive structure. Second, if an organization wishes to accomplish its plans, the incentive structures inherent in the workplace must be consistent with the organization's desired outcomes. If they are not, people's energies will not be directed toward the plans but toward those activities for which the individuals are rewarded. Third, it is possible to determine, in at least general terms, the incentive pattern of people working within academia—namely, faculty and staff. Each of these assumptions flows directly from modern day economic theory. Incentive planning views the college or university as an economic organization, comprised of individuals who behave in a manner which reflects their incentive structures.

Incentive planning, as described by Hoenack and Berg in Chapter Five, may be characterized as a "hands-off" approach to planning. While some planning approaches (for example, formal democratic style) work toward agreement on the particular ideas and programs which will be implemented, Incentive Planning establishes a reward system and then leaves the individual units to their own devices. If the institution wishes to increase certain activities (such as outside research funding), then the incentive system must be changed to motivate additional activity in this arena (released time, indirect cost recovery). How faculty go about securing additional research funds is left to each faculty member or department. Instead of debating alternative programs for raising additional research money and then agreeing on an approach, the responsibility of administration is only to establish the reward mechanisms. Faculty and departments are then free to respond to this new incentive in any way they choose. This approach to college and university planning builds on the belief that there are many different ways to arrive at the desired goal, and it is most effective if individuals are free to design and select their own alternatives.

In this hands-off approach to planning the college or university still must have firm grasp on its desired outcomes—its mission and goals. Without this, there will be no criteria on which to formulate incentives. Even with incentive planning in place, the institution must set up mechanisms for determining its overall mission and goals. This determination could include input from faculty, students, administration, trustees, and community representatives. With participation from many constituencies, the institution's primary thrust could be determined. Then, it is the responsibility of administration to establish incentives which are responsive to this institutional mission.

If incentive planning is to succeed, two potential challenges must be overcome. First, it must be demonstrated that in fact administrators know or can learn what motivates faculty and academic departments. This knowledge is essential if meaningful incentives are to be established. Second, incentive planning requires operational statistics and cost information different from those collected by most colleges and universities. If every unit is free to operate its own—"maximize its profit," in the parlance of economics—cost information must be available so that cross charges can be made (Zemsky, Porter, and Oedel, 1978). Operational data must be collected to reflect the effect of the incentives so that they may be modified when necessary.

Incentive planning is an intriguing approach to academic planning. It combines many of the prerequisites of effective academic governance. It facilitates the separation of mission and goal determination from administration. It leaves each unit and each faculty member free to determine how they will respond to the prescribed incentives. And it relegates the development of specific incentives, an administrative responsibility, to the administrators. Moreover, incentive planning recognizes an obvious yet important characteristic of organizational change: the reward structure within any organization must be consistent with its desired outcomes, if change is to occur. Although used in some private institutions and written about extensively, incentive planning has thus far been overlooked by most of the postsecondary education community.

Formal Democratic

This planning style, although not covered specifically in any one of the preceding chapters, is included here because of its wide appeal and use today in colleges and universities. (Variants of this approach are described in detail by Kieft, Amijo, and Bucklew, 1978, and Parekh, 1975). The terminology *formal democratic* was coined by the author to reflect two specific characteristics. This planning approach may be described as *formal* because it specifies a sequence of events and a schedule for each cycle of planning. It is termed *democratic* because it typically is a comprehensive planning process that requires all departments to submit their plans to the college and all colleges to submit their plans to central administration. These plans may be in many different forms including goals and objectives, performance objectives, and descriptions of program intent. Plans are assessed by succeedingly higher levels of administration and eventually a plan is agreed upon for the department, the college and the university.

The process builds on the creativity and vision of each department. It is assumed that by simultaneously considering the plans of each unit, those ideas best suited to the institution will emerge. This planning style build on the norms of academic governance, which look to individual faculty members for ideas, and proceeds through a hierarchical process of consultation.

Formal democratic planning offers some obvious contrasts to incentive planning. In democratic planning specific plans for new programs and strategies for implementation may be part of the planning process. This style also offers a mechanism for arriving at institution-wide goals. It assumes that commitment for accomplishing plans can be built by means of open participation in a planning process. It also assumes that administrators have the power to ensure that plans are accomplished. Typically this would be done through selective resource allocation which reflects the agreed upon institutional and department plans. Performance may then be assessed *ex post facto* against the plans outlined.

In contrast, incentive planning begins with a known institutional mission and institutional goals, and sets out to modify the incentives to accomplish these goals. Specific programs to realize goal accomplishment are not predetermined. Instead, the departments and people comprising the institution respond in any ways that seem most appropriate, given the incentive structure.

In contrast to the other four approaches reviewed in this chapter, formal democratic planning focuses on a broad, open process aimed at comprehensively involving the institution. It can begin with a needs assessment; it can build on program data; and it could include the formulation of new incentives to accomplish plans. Its appeal within postsecondary education is due to its openness and consistency with norms of academic governance. Whether it can live up to its expectations remains to be seen.

Summary

There are a variety of styles that can be used to plan academic programs. Some of these approaches are centuries old and would not be termed "planning" by many contemporary theorists. This sourcebook has singled out for detailed treatment some of those planning approaches which seem applicable to the 1980s. Clearly the older, more individually based program planning approaches (such as entrepreneurial) must continue to be used at the level of the individual course and within the single academic program. However, the conditions facing postsecondary education in this decade call for institutional planning styles which are (1) more comprehensive, (2) more systematic, (3) more public, (4) more regular, and (5) more expansive than the current norms of academic governance.

More Comprehensive. In a contracting environment difficult choices must be made among competing alternatives, and only with a simultaneous examination of all possible choices can the most effective decisions be made. During periods of growth, it seems less necessary to contrast program alternatives, one against the other.

More Systematic. In a society continually expanding its technological capabilities, there is mounting pressure to make decisions more systematically. It is expected that quantitative indicators will be collected to inform decision makers about competing alternatives. Goals will be developed, put in priority order, and assessed for productivity. As difficult choices have to be made, administrators will increasingly rely on quantitative indicators that they can defend publicly. Whether such methodologies are used to rationalize a subjective judgment or are actually employed to make an "objective" decision is always open to question. Nevertheless, the expectation is that with improved planning, decisions will be made more systematically.

More Public. With growing distrust of organizational leaders and the need to cut back on program size, there is mounting pressure to reveal the decision-making process. Faculty demand that criteria for retrenchment and reallocation decisions be debated publicly before the actual process of pruning begins. Data privacy laws, while protecting the individual, may classify institutional planning documents as public information. Thus, not only faculty and students but any concerned citizen may review planning materials. Architects of planning processes will come to recognize the increased credibility which results from opening up the process.

More Regular. To complement the need to be more comprehensive and systematic, planning styles are increasingly designed around a fixed schedule of events. The formal planning process is repeated annually or biennially, for without this it is difficult to ensure its comprehensiveness or to justify that it is regular. A planning calender, like budgeting, recognizes the importance of the activity and does not allow the insitution to ignore the regular need to plan. In a rapidly changing environment with a complex set of interdependencies it is necessary to "take stock" frequently and reassess the status of the institution's academic programs.

More Expansive. Newer academic planning styles will also extend the span of years considered in decisions. Instead of examining a proposed program in the context of only today's environment, academic administration will increasingly look into the future—perhaps across a number of different environments—to assess the desirability of inaugurating a program. In order to be more systematic and comprehensive, it is necessary to consider events across an extended period of time. The countervailing force, however, is the ever more rapidly changing environment which makes a gaze into an increasingly fragile crystal ball more and more difficult. A recognition of these contradictory phenomena reinforces the need to become more systematic, more comprehensive, and more regular in planning styles.

These demands will leave the academic administrator in a precarious position. Many of these characteristics have the potential for eroding academic freedom and the autonomy of the individual faculty member. Undoubtedly the 1980s will necessitate a more intrusive, more management-oriented form of planning. Yet if this is done at the sacrifice of faculty freedom, colleges and universities will be no better than public agencies and bureaucracies.

The most effective academic administrators will be those who can balance these many demands. Cognizance of the various styles in which academic programs might be planned will be necessary if institutional decision makers are going to respond in an effective manner. Certainly, no single planning style is best. Each approach has its unique strengths and weaknesses. Most importantly, the effective administrator will select characteristics from each style that are adaptable to one's own environment.

Although these planning approaches have been treated independently in this sourcebook, it is important to recognize that styles can be linked and that there is often a natural sequencing of them. For example, understanding the current status of programs may be a necessary first step, building on program data. Then a needs assessment might be conducted to develop new ideas for programs. Finally, a retrenchment and reallocation process might be initiated to generate funds for these new programs.

Regardless of which style or series of approaches is used, the single most important factor in moving an institution toward more effective planning is insightful, firm, imaginative academic leadership. Momentum for planning can be created and maintained only the the institution's academic leaders. They must understand organizational change and they must sustain it. And most important, their day-to-day decisions must build on the decisions made in the planning process. Planning will become effective only when institutional leaders continually demonstrate a cognizance of plans and by example demonstrate the necessity of making decisions which are consistent with the institution's articulated aspirations.

Finally, there is the inescapable and perhaps most important conclusion: any approach to academic planning and decision making requires a clear vision of the institution's academic priorities. Some of the styles discussed in this sourcebook (for example, incentive planning) assume the existence of these priorities, whereas other styles establish a mechanism for developing them (formal democratic). There is no predetermined set of academic values or list of programs at the core of an institution. Each institution must decide on its educational philosophy and core programs. Because an institution is moving through time, setting academic priorities is a never-ending process which balances the needs of the society against the mission of the institution and the available program resources.

We must retain at all times an understanding of the unique role which colleges and universities play in society. In the United States, this role will most likely be undergoing tough cross-examination during the 1980s. Effective approaches to academic program planning can assist us through this period so that postsecondary education enters the 1990s with renewed vigor and still higher quality.

References

Kieft, R. N., Armijo, F., and Bucklew, N. S. *A Handbook for Institutional Academic and Program Planning: From Idea to Implementation.* Boulder, Colo.: National Center for Higher Education Management Systems, 1978.

Parekh, S. B. *Long-Range Planning: An Institutionwide Approach to Increasing Academic Vitality.* New Rochelle, N.Y.: Change Magazine Press, 1975.

Zemsky, R., Porter, R., and Oedel, L. P. "Decentralized Planning: To Share Responsibility." *Educational Record,* Summer 1978.

Richard B. Heydinger is assistant to the vice-president for academic affairs at the University of Minnesota; he is on partial leave for three years as a Kellogg Fellow to study higher education planning and its relationship to long-range planning in other sectors of society.

Sources of further information are presented.

Further Sources on Academic Planning

Richard B. Heydinger

The term *academic program planning* has been widely used in the higher education literature to refer to a number of distinct planning activities. In some writings it refers to all planning conducted by the institution. Since colleges and universities are academic institutions, their planning is termed *academic planning*. A more precise terminology for this concept is institutional planning. In other publications, discussion is focused on the skills and background required for a liberal education. This literature focuses on the student as the unit of analysis and debates liberal education requirements. Another portion of the publications on academic program planning inventories the variety of pedagogical techniques available to those who would like to breathe new life into the curriculum. Other articles and books discuss the governance of the academic department and the forces which can lead to curricular change. These latter writings could be included within the definition of academic program planning used in this chapter. However, many of them are more accurately characterized as part of the writing on instructional or faculty development.

As curious readers approach the topic of academic planning (as defined in this volume), it is often most useful to start with the general and proceed to the specific. A most lucid overview dealing with many different facets of planning is Michael's book, *On Learning to Plan and Planning to Learn* (1973). Although not written specifically for a postsecondary education audience, his notions of organizational learning and acceptance of error provide a new and much needed perspective for the administrator or institutional researcher responsible for implementing a new planning process. To give a reasonably objective view of the topic, Shuck (1977) has written a witty, literary essay that both criticizes and supports planning activities. His provocative article is most useful as a discussion topic for a group of faculty and administrators working together on planning. People's preferences for planning styles can be quickly separated when they react to Schmidtlein's (1974) insightful analysis of the two decision-making styles that have emerged in higher education. The tension implied in this article will undoubtedly emerge in any institution attempting to introduce a comprehensive planning style.

One of the most difficult yet fundamental aspects of academic planning is setting academic priorities and weighing them against "academic values." In a practical yet conceptually rigorous approach, Shirley and Volkwein (1978) describe their method for arriving at a set of academic program priorities. Their framework has been most useful to me on a number of occasions. Also, Fuller (1976) effectively reiterates the importance of academic values.

For readers seeking a how-to-do-it methodology for academic planning, at least three good references exist. Kieft and his NCHEMS colleagues describe the experiences of four institutions (1978) and their attempts to inaugurate new planning processes. A companion monograph by Kieft (1978) builds on the findings from these experiences and lays out a model academic planning process. Parekh (1975) offers even more detail by providing forms and suggested procedures. Finally, an excellent publication combining a thorough conceptual framework with specific recommendations and forms is Sturner's *Action Planning on the Campus*. This fifty-page monograph is a good reference work for all institutional researchers.

A major point of departure from the comprehensive approach to planning is the decentralized one labeled "economic incentives." A practical overview of the real world implications of moving to this planning style is provided by Zemsky, Porter, and Oedel (1978) as they describe their experiences at the University of Pennsylvania. Hoenack (1977) and associates (1974) have written two articles that suggest ways of using economic incentives at the college or departmental level. These articles are complex, rigorous discussions of the topic. They are well organized and must be read by anyone seriously interested in this approach. In a provocative article, Cyert (1978) speaks in nontechnical terms to many issues related to economic incentives.

Readers looking for procedural guidance are advised to consult Michael (1973) for a general perspective and Haas (1976), Poland and Arns (1978), Mims (1979), and Norris (1978) for more specific suggestions.

References

Cyert, R. M. "The Management of Universities of Constant or Decreasing Size." *Public Administration Review*, 1978, *38*, 344-349.
Fuller, B. "A Framework for Academic Planning." *Journal of Higher Education*, 1976, *47*, 65-77.
Haas, R. M. "Integrating Academic, Fiscal, and Facilities Planning." *Planning for Higher Education*, 1976, *5*, 2-5.
Hoenack, S. A. "Direct and Incentive Planning Within a University." *Socio-Economic Planning Science*, 1977, *11*, 191-204.
Hoenack, S. A., and others. "University Planning, Decentralization, and Resource Allocation." *Socio-Economic Planning Science*, 1977, *11, 191*-204.
Kieft, R. N. *Academic Planning: Four Institutional Case Studies.* Boulder, Colo.: NCHEMS, 1978.
Kieft, R. N., Armijo, F., and Bucklew, N. S. *A Handbook for Institutional Academic and Program Planning: From Idea to Implementation.* Boulder, Colo.: NCHEMS, 1978.
Michael, D. N. *On Learning to Plan and Planning to Learn: The Social Psychology of Changing Toward Future-Responsive Societal Learning.* San Francisco: Jossey-Bass, 1973.
Mims, R. S. "Facilitating Pervasive Planning: Multi-Level Institutional Planning." Paper delivered at AIR Forum, San Diego, California, 1979.
Norris, D. M. "Matching Planning Activities to the Needs of the Organization." Paper delivered at Society for College and University Planning, Kansas City, July 1979.
Parekh, S. B. *Long-Range Planning.* New Rochelle, N.Y.: Change Magazine Press, 1975.
Poland, W., and Arns, R. G. "Characteristics of Successful Planning Activities." *Planning for Higher Education*, 1978, *7*, 1-6.
Schmidtlein, F. A. "Decision Process Paradigms in Education." *Educational Record*, May 1974, pp. 4-11.
Shirley, R. C., and Volkwein, J. F. "Establishing Academic Program Priorities." *Journal of Higher Education*, 1978, *49*, 472-488.
Shuck, E. C. "The New Planning and an Old Pragmatism." *Journal of Higher Education*, 1977, *49*, 594-602.
Sturner, W. F. *Action Planning on the Campus.* Washington, D.C.: American Association of State Colleges and Universities, 1974.
Zemsky, R., Porter, R., and Oedel, L. P. "Decentralized Planning: To Share Responsibility." *Educational Record*, 1978, *59*, 229-253.

Richard B. Heydinger is assistant to the vice-president for academic affairs at the University of Minnesota.

Index

A

Academic planning, 1-3, 7-8, 98; and budgeting combined, 29-32; central issues of, 106-108; literature on, 111-113; styles of, 3-7. *See also* Planning
Academic planning committees, incentive behavior of, 74-76
Academic programs, 2
Action Planning on Campus, 112
Adams, K. A., 21-22
Administration, and planning style, 4, 53. *See also* Deans; Staffing
Annual Evaluation and Report (AER), 28-29; problems with, 32, 49; process, 33-34, 51; prototype, 29-30; refinements in, 30-32; sample forms for, 35-48
Armijo, F., 105, 109, 112-113
Arns, R. G., 113
Arrow, K. J., 74-75, 93
Association for Instructional Research, 9n
Association of American Universities, Data Exchange, 92
Aulepp, L., 21, 23

B

Baird, L. L., 19, 23
Baumheier, E. C., 10, 23
Bear, D. V. T., 84, 93
Beatty, P. T., 22-23
Becker, W. E., Jr., 87, 93-94
Berg, D. J., 7, 73-95, 104
Bergstrom, R. C., 88, 93
Bishop, J., 88, 93
Boggs, J. H., 65, 67-68, 72
Borcherding, T. E., 88, 93
Boyd, H. W., 20, 23
Bradshaw, J., 18, 23
Breneman, D. W., 87-88, 90n, 93
Brown, B. W., 21, 23
Bucklew, N. S., 105, 109, 112-113
Budgeting: data planning style of, 29-31; with evaluation, 28-32; with evaluation and planning, 33-34, 49, 52; and incentive systems, 81-84; and planning decisions, 6; research needs in, 90-91; responsibility systems of, 84-86. *See also* Reallocation
Burton, J. K., 13, 21, 23

C

California, University of, budgeting system, 87-88
Central Florida Community Colleges Consortium, 21, 23
Change plan, 32, 34, 41n, 42-44, 48
Cheit, E. F., 57, 72
Clotfelter, C. T., 88, 93
Clurman, M., 89, 93
Coffing, R. T., 10-11, 21, 23
Committees, incentive behavior of, 74-76
Communities, needs assessment for, 14-16, 18, 21
Community colleges, planning by, 5
Computers, 6, 52. *See also* Data; Program data planning style
Constrained maximization behavior, 78-79, 82. *See also* Incentives
Continuing education, research needs in, 89-90
Cook, R., 84, 94
Cooper, E. M., 21, 24
Coordinating boards, and planning, 4
Cootner, P. H., 84, 93
Craven, E., 5, 8
Curriculum committee, and planning, 4
Cyert, R. M., 58, 72, 112-113

D

Daniere, A., 84, 93
Data: handling of, 51-53; for incentive planning, 104; in needs assessment, 19-21, 99-100; and privacy, 107; for reallocation, 72. *See also* Annual Evaluation and Report (AER); Program data planning style
Davies, B., 92, 94
Deacon, R. T., 88, 93
Deans, annual evaluation and report for, 29-30, 40, 46, 48, 50, 53

115

Delworth, E., 21, 23
Demand: expressed vs. effective, 99; legislative, 91; in planning, 83-84, 88. *See also* Needs
Departments: annual evaluation and report for, 29-30, 35-49; planning focus of, 2-3
Discretionary funds, 84-85
Dressel, P., 30-33, 55
Drucker, P. F., 2, 8
Dunworth, J., 84, 94

E

EDUCOM financial planning model, 49, 102
English, F. W., 21, 23
Enrollments, in incentive systems, 88, 91-92
Entrepreneurial planning style, 3-5, 106
Evaluation, annual cycles of, 33, 51; and budgeting combined, 28-32; with budgeting and planning, 33-34, 49, 52. *See also* Annual Evaluation and Report (AER)
Ewing, D. W., 8
Excellence Fund (Oklahoma State University), 71-72; criteria and priorities for, 67; design and phase-in of, 65-66; Priority Fund comparison, 69-71; problems, strengths and results of, 67-68; purposes and rationale of, 65; reallocation process, 66-67

F

Faculty: and planning styles, 3-5; research and publication activities of, 31, 35; workload of, 37-39. *See also* Research; Staffing
Feldstein, M., 88, 94
"Fiscal distress," incentive planning and, 89-90. *See also* Retrenchment
Flexibility plan, 32, 34, 45-46, 49
Formal democratic planning style, 3-7, 97-98, 104-106, 108
Freeman, T. M., 6, 27-55, 100, 102
Fuller, B., 112-113

G

Gollattscheck, J., 21, 23
Goodman, R. P., 88, 93
Gotsick, P., 21, 23
Governing boards, and planning, 4

Gray, R. W., 21, 23
Groups: decision making by, 74-78; needs assessment for, 14-16
Growth conditions: budgeting for, 32, 34, 42-44, 48, 102, 106; reallocation for, 57n, 64-71

H

Haas, R. M., 113
Hamilton, D. L., 21, 23
Heller, G. A., 10, 23
Heydinger, R. B., 1-8, 97-113
Higher Education Management Institute, 21, 23
Hodson, W. A., 21, 23
Hoenack, S. A., 7, 73-95, 104, 112-113
Hoepfner, R., 21, 23
Hutchinson, T. E., 10-11, 21, 23

I

Incentives, 4-7, 73-74; individual and group, 74-78; instructionally related, 87-89; and planning decisions, 78-84, 103-105, 108, 112; in public institutions, 85-86; for research activities, 86-87, 89; research needs in, 88-92; research overview of, 84-88; specific and overall, 79-82, 87; structuring of, 76-81
Incremental budgeting, 4-6. *See also* Reallocation
Institutional goals: and incentive systems, 78-79; and planning, 53-55, 104-106
Institutional research office, 100-101

J

Jackman, R., 84, 94
Jackson, G. A., 88, 94
Jedamus, P., 8

K

Kahn, A., 2, 8
Karman, T. A., 57n, 65, 67-68, 72
Kaufman, R. A., 21, 23
Keim, W. A., 21, 23
Kieft, R. N., 105, 109, 112-113
Kinnick, M. K., 18, 21, 23-24
Klein, S. P., 21, 24
Knowledge development planning style, 3-5, 97

L

Lave, J., 22, 24
Layard, R., 84, 94
League of California Cities, 21, 24
Lenning, O. T., 5, 9-25, 98-100
Levine, C. H., 57, 72
Lewis, D. R., 87, 94
Lewis, J. L., 21, 24
Lumsden, K. G., 93-94

M

McCaslin, N. L., 22, 24
Mager, R. R., 22, 24
Management information systems, 6. *See also* Data; Program data planning style
Market factors. *See* Demand; Incentives; Needs assessment; Outputs; Profit
Maslow, A. H., 18, 24
"Median voter model," 88, 91
Merrill, P. F., 13, 21, 23
Michael, D. N., 112-113
Michigan, University of at Ann Arbor, 6; Budget Priorities Committee, 60, 63; Committee on Budget Administration, 60, 63; General Fund, 59, 61; Office of Academic Affairs, 59-64; Priority Fund, 58-64, 69-71
Michigan State University, 27-28, 102; Annual Evaluation and Review process, 6, 28-55; budget reduction planning phase, 49-50; evaluation and budgeting phase, 28-32; Office of Institutional Research, 28, 31, 49; planning, evaluation and budgeting phase, 33-49; planning lessons learned at, 51-55
Miller, L. S., 88, 94
Mims, R. S., 6, 57-72, 101-103, 113
Minnesota, University of, 85
Mooney Problem Checklist, 18
Morgan, J. M., 21, 24
Mortimer, K. P., 58, 70, 72
Mueller, D. C., 75, 94
Murray, H. A., 18, 24

N

National Center for Higher Education Management Systems (NCHEMS), Outcomes Structure, 14-18
National Institute of Education, 90, 94

Needs, 5-6; administrative, 21; characterizing of, 13-19; of communities, 14-16, 18, 21; concept of, 9-13, 18; in continuing education, 21; course level, 21; curricular, 21-22; environmental, 21; goal related, 22; of handicapped students, 21; hierarchy of, 18; outcome types in terms of, 17; performance related, 22; social, 18; state level, 21-22; vocational and occupational, 21. *See also* Demand
Needs assessment, 3-6, 9-10, 98-100, 108; audiences for, 14-17; conduct of, 19-22; focus of, 14-19; models of, 21-22
Needs surveys, 19-21
Nerlove, M., 87, 94
New Jersey State Department of Education, 21, 24
Nobay, A. R., 94
Norman, A. L., 84, 94
Norris, D. M., 113

O

Oedel, L. P., 84, 94, 104, 109, 112-113
Oklahoma State University, 6, 58; Academic Affairs and Research Office, 66; Excellence Fund, 57n, 64-71; Presidential Challenge Grant, 66; Vice President's and Dean's Incentive Grant, 66
On Learning to Plan and Planning to Learn, 112-113
Organizations, needs assessment for, 14-16
Outcomes: measurement of, 20; and reward structures, 105; types of, 16-19. *See also* Incentives; Outputs
Outcomes Structure (NCHEMS), 14-18
Outputs, and planning policy, 81-83

P

Pagels, C. F., 18, 21, 24
Parekh, S. B., 105, 109, 112-113
Parkin, M., 94
Parsons, T., 18, 24
Pennsylvania, University of, 84, 94, 112
Peterson, M., 8
Peterson, R. E., 22, 24
Pfeffer, J., 90n-91n, 94
Pipe, P., 22, 24

Planning, 2; with budgeting and evaluation, 33-34, 49, 52; comprehensiveness of, 106, 112; cycles of, 107; goals of, 54; growth oriented, 32, 34, 42-46; and incentive systems, 78-88; institutional level, 53-55; needs in, 106-108; procedures in, 113; public aspects of, 107; reduction oriented, 32, 34, 45-46, 49-50; research needs in, 89-92; styles of, 97-98, 108; systematic, 106-107; time span of, 107-108. *See also* Academic planning; Annual Evaluation and Review (AER); Formal democratic planning style; Incentives; Needs assessment; Program data planning style; Reallocation

Poland, W., 113
Porter, R., 84, 94, 104, 109, 112-113
Priority Fund (University of Michigan-Ann Arbor), 58-59; allocation criteria, 61; comparison with Excellence Fund, 69-71; design and phase-in of, 59-60; future of, 64; problems, strengths and results of, 62-64; purposes and rationale of, 59; reallocation process, 60-62
Priority Fund, 59, 72
Problem focused planning style, 4, 97
Profit, and planning policy, 80-87
Program data planning style, 3-6, 97, 100-101, 108. *See also* Annual Evaluation and Review (AER)
Program development fund, 4
Program review planning style, 4-5
Public institutions, budgeting for, 85-86
Publications, and planning evaluation, 31, 35
Putnam, C. E., 21, 24

R

Radner, R., 88, 94
Read, B., 21, 24
Reallocation, 58, 101-103, 108; comparison of methods, 69-72; for declining income, 58-64; factors affecting, 70-72; growth oriented, 64-78; public aspects of, 107. *See also* Excellence fund; Priority Fund
Reder, M. W., 84, 94
Reece, W. S., 88, 94
Research: basic and applied, 83-84, 87; cost study needs, 92; and incentive systems, 78, 82, 86-87, 89; and planning evaluation, 31

Resource Planning and Excellence, 62, 72
Responsibility budgeting systems, 84-86; research incentives in, 86-87
Retrenchment: incentive planning for, 89-90; planning for, 4, 6, 9-10, 32, 34, 45-46, 49. *See also* Reallocation
Rewards structures. *See* Incentives
Robl, R. M., 65, 67-68, 72

S

Salamon, L. D., 84, 94
Salancik, G. R., 90n-91n, 94
Schmidtlein, F. A., 112-113
Schultz, T. P., 86, 94
Scriven, J., 10-12, 24
Selgas, J. W., 21, 25
Shapiro, H. T., 62, 72
Shirley, R. C., 112-113
Shook, L. L., 22, 25
Shuck, E. C., 112-113
Simon, L. A. K., 30-33, 55
Simpson, W. A., 6, 27-55, 100, 102
Smith, H. K., 21, 25
Staffing, planning and budgeting for, 35-50, 69. *See also* Faculty
Stigler, G. J., 74, 94
Strauss, J. C., 84, 94
Students: financial aid needs of, 22; information needs of, 21; needs assessment for, 14-20
Sturner, W. F., 112-113
Support units, annual evaluation reports of, 29

T

Taxonomy of Information Needs of Prospective Students, 18
Taxonomy of Social Need, 18
Taylor, E. N., 12, 25
Tierney, M. L., 58, 70, 72
Tucker, K. D., 21, 25

U

Uhl, V. P., 24
Updegrove, D. A., 49, 55

V

Van Dyk, J., 88, 93
Verry, D., 92, 94
Volkwein, J. F., 112-113

W

Watson, D. S., 74, 94
Weathersby, G. B., 88, 94
Weiler, W. C., 88, 94
Weinschrott, D., 88, 94
Westfall, R., 20, 23
Witkin, B. R., 21, 25

Y

Yale University, 86

Z

Zemsky, R., 84, 94, 104, 109, 112–113

New Directions Quarterly Sourcebooks

New Directions for Institutional Research is one of several distinct series of quarterly sourcebooks published by Jossey-Bass. The sourcebooks in each series are designed to serve both as *convenient compendiums* of the latest knowledge and practical experience on their topics and as *long-life reference tools.*

One-year, four-sourcebook subscriptions for each series cost $18 for individuals (when paid by personal check) and $30 for institutions, libraries, and agencies. Single copies of earlier sourcebooks are available at $6.95 each *prepaid* (or $7.95 each when *billed*).

A complete listing is given below of current and past sourcebooks in the *New Directions for Institutional Research* series. The titles and editors-in-chief of the other series are also listed. To subscribe, or to receive further information, write: New Directions Subscriptions, Jossey-Bass Inc., Publishers, 433 California Street, San Francisco, California 94104.

New Directions for Institutional Research
Marvin W. Peterson, Editor-in-Chief

1974:
1. *Evaluating Institutions for Accountability,* Howard Bowen
2. *Assessing Faculty Effort,* James Doi
3. *Toward Affirmative Action,* Lucy Sells
4. *Organizing Nontraditional Study,* Samuel Baskin

1975:
5. *Evaluating Statewide Boards,* Robert Berdahl
6. *Assuring Academic Progress Without Growth,* Allan Cartter
7. *Responding to Changing Human Resource Needs,* Paul Heist, Jonathan Warren
8. *Measuring and Increasing Academic Productivity,* Robert A. Wallhaus

1976:
9. *Assessing Computer-Based Systems Models,* Thomas Mason
10. *Examining Departmental Management,* James Montgomery, James Smart
11. *Allocating Resources Among Departments,* Paul Dressel, Lou Anna Kimsey Simon
12. *Benefiting from Interinstitutional Research,* Marvin W. Peterson

1977:
13. *Applying Analytic Methods to Planning and Management,* David Hopkins, Roger Schroeder
14. *Protecting Individual Rights to Privacy in Higher Education,* Alton Taylor
15. *Appraising Information Needs of Decision Makers,* Carl Adams
16. *Increasing the Public Accountability of Higher Education,* John Folger

1978: 17. *Analyzing and Constructing Cost,* Meredith A. Gonyea
       18. *Employing Part-Time Faculty,* David Leslie
       19. *Using Goals in Research Planning,* Robert H. Fenske
       20. *Evaluating Faculty Performance and Vitality,* Wayne Kirschling
1979: 21. *Developing a Total Marketing Plan,* John A. Lucas
       22. *Examining New Trends in Administrative Computing,*
           E. Michael Staman
       23. *Professional Development for Institutional Research,*
           Robert G. Cope
       24. *Planning Rational Retrenchment,* Alfred L. Cooke
1980: 25. *The Impact of Student Financial Aid on Institutions,*
           Joe B. Henry
       26. *The Autonomy of Public Colleges,* Paul L. Dressel
       27. *Academic Program Evaluation,* Eugene C. Craven

New Directions for Child Development
William Damon, Editor-in-Chief

New Directions for College Learning Assistance
Kurt V. Lauridsen, Editor-in-Chief

New Directions for Community Colleges
Arthur M. Cohen, Editor-in-Chief
Florence B. Brawer, Associate Editor

New Directions for Continuing Education
Alan B. Knox, Editor-in-Chief

New Directions for Exceptional Children
James J. Gallagher, Editor-in-Chief

New Directions for Experiential Learning
Pamela J. Tate, Editor-in-Chief
Morris T. Keeton, Consulting Editor

New Directions for Higher Education
JB Lon Hefferlin, Editor-in-Chief

New Directions for Institutional Advancement
A. Westley Rowland, Editor-in-Chief

New Directions for Mental Health Services
H. Richard Lamb, Editor-in-Chief

New Directions for Methodology of Social and Behavioral Science
Donald W. Fiske, Editor-in-Chief

New Directions for Program Evaluation
Scarvia B. Anderson, Editor-in-Chief

New Directions for Student Services
Ursula Delworth and Gary R. Hanson, Editors-in-Chief

New Directions for Teaching and Learning
Kenneth E. Eble and John Noonan, Editors-in-Chief

New Directions for Testing and Measurement
William B. Schrader, Editor-in-Chief

STATEMENT OF OWNERSHIP, MANAGEMENT, AND CIRCULATION
(Required by 39 U.S.C. 3685)

1. Title of Publication: New Directions for Institutional Research. A. Publication number: USPS 098-830. 2. Date of filing: September 29, 1980. 3. Frequency of issue: quarterly. A. Number of issues published annually: four. B. Annual subscription price: $30 institutions; $18 individuals. 4. Location of known office of publication: 433 California Street, San Francisco (San Francisco County), California 94104. 5. Location of the headquarters or general business offices of the publishers: 433 California Street, San Francisco (San Francisco County), California 94104. 6. Names and addresses of publisher, editor, and managing editor: publisher—Jossey-Bass Inc., Publishers, 433 California Street, San Francisco, California 94104; editor—Marvin Peterson, Center for the Study of Higher Education, University of Michigan, Ann Arbor, MI 48109; managing editor—JB Lon Hefferlin, 433 California Street, San Francisco, California 94104. 7. Owner: Jossey-Bass Inc., Publishers, 433 California Street, San Francisco, California 94104. 8. Known bondholders, mortgages, and other security holders owning or holding 1 percent or more of total amount of bonds, mortgages, or other securities: same as No. 7. 10. Extent and nature of circulation: (Note: first number indicates the average number of copies of each issue during the preceding twelve months; the second number indicates the actual number of copies published nearest to filing date.) A. Total number of copies printed (net press run): 2472, 2515. B. Paid circulation, 1) Sales through dealers and carriers, street vendors, and counter sales: 85, 40. 2) Mail subscriptions: 1058, 668. C. Total paid circulation: 1143, 708. D. Free distribution by mail, carrier, or other means (samples, complimentary, and other free copies): 125, 125. E. Total distribution (sum of C and D): 1268, 883. F. Copies not distributed, 1) Office use, left over, unaccounted, spoiled after printing: 1204, 1682. 2) Returns from news agents: 0, 0. G. Total (sum of E, F1, and 2—should equal net press run shown in A): 2472, 2515.

I certify that the statements made by me above are correct and complete.

JOHN R. WARD
Vice-President